W Procter

The Management And Treatment of the Horse in the Stable, Field,

And on the Road

W Procter

The Management And Treatment of the Horse in the Stable, Field, And on the Road

ISBN/EAN: 9783744732901

Printed in Europe, USA, Canada, Australia, Japan

Cover: Foto ©Andreas Hilbeck / pixelio.de

More available books at **www.hansebooks.com**

THE

MANAGEMENT & TREATMENT

OF THE

HORSE

IN THE

STABLE, FIELD, AND ON THE ROAD.

BY A STUD-GROOM.

LONDON :

THE LONDON LITERARY SOCIETY,

376 STRAND, W.

1882.

NORWICH :
"ARGUS" PRINTING WORKS, ST. GILES'.

LONDON :
81 FLEET STREET, E.C.

THE MANAGEMENT

AND

TREATMENT OF THE HORSE.

"Happy he who studies nature's laws,
Through effects can trace the certain cause."—VIRGIL.

I THINK I cannot do better to begin this short
treatise than by pointing out some of the evils the
horse has to suffer in consequence of the ignorance
displayed by the architect who first draws the plan of
the stable. I will endeavour to show in a few simple
words the great faults in nearly every stable I have been
in for the last twenty years, some of which have been
the best in England.

The first defect to be noticed is the floor. In the
first place the floor of the stable is always made high in
front of the horse's head, and slopes down low to his hind
feet. This, I contend, is unnatural, and therefore wrong.
The stable should always be made with the hind part at
least one inch higher than the fore part. Some people
may object to this on the ground that the water will all
run under the horse and cause a great waste of litter.

This may be easily avoided by placing one grate in the centre of the stall near the horse's fore feet, about four feet from the wall at the manger, and another grate in the centre of the stall, in a line with the gutter at the end of the stall. The question will naturally be asked, why would you make this alteration which is in just contra-distinction to the most approved plans, drawn in the present day? I refer the enquirers in quest of informa-tion, to the fields and open country. Let him study the horse there, and he will always see it when standing at its ease, (and it will not stand still at all if it is not comfortable) with its hind feet on the highest ground. I am speaking of sound horses, and this fact is quite in keeping with the structure of the horse. If we will but take the trouble to study its anotomy we shall then find, by placing the horse in that unnatural position with his fore feet on the highest ground, that we throw undue pressure constantly upon the muscles of the belly, causing the *colon* or large gut to fall upon the *cæcum*, thereby preventing to a great extent that freedom of action which is so necessary to that organ, to enable all the substances taken in to re-ascend into the *caput coli*, and to pass on to the *rectum*. Another great evil arising out of it is the pain it causes the animal by causing a great strain on the *flexor* tendon, and the back sinews of the legs, no doubt leading to many of the cases of lameness by windgall and rupture of the sheeth of the tendons, commonly called broken down. I once had a very bad case of break-down, though the animal had not been out of the stable from the Saturday morn-ing until I found it on Monday morning dead lame, and

1 could not account for it being done in no other way than by slipping on the sloping pavement. I was called a short time ago to see a horse belonging to a carman, which in shaking itself in the stable slipped and fell, breaking both knees, one very severely; this was another victim to a false system of paving. If you go into any stable that is paved with the fore part the highest, you will find all the horses hang back to the extent of their rack chains, or stand crossways in their stalls, to try to raise their hind feet into a natural position. Go again into a stable of loose boxes that have a grate in the centre of the box, and what do we find ? Every horse with his fore feet in the drain or lowest part of the box, while his haunches are on the highest ground. These facts should be enough to convince any-one that the present system is altogether wrong.

LIGHT.

"Stand on one side and let God's light and sunshine fall upon me and my horse," are the words I should like to impress upon every builder. Go through all the stables in town and country and see how few have had due attention for light bestowed upon them by the builder. We find small windows, and not one half of them will open, and where they are put they are placed in the very spot to give the smallest amount of light possible. Whereas the windows in every stable should be large, and open from top and bottom, and should be looking to the east if possible, and the horses' heads to the west, so that the sun may shine into the stable as soon as it rises in the morning, spreading its light into every corner of the stable. The front of the stall before the horse's head should never be white, but stone or dark colour, white having as bad an effect upon the eye as a dark stable. If anyone doubt this let him look upon a piece of white paper when the sun is shining, and judge for himself. Again, look upon any bright colour in a strong light for a few seconds, and then turn and look at the blue sky or any other object, and the eye will reflect in a different form the object first looked upon, and show it distinctly upon the second substance. If looking upon white or any bright colour in a strong light for a few seconds has such an effect upon the optic nerve of the human being, what effect has it upon the horse, that is compelled to look upon it for hours together day after day ? I have no doubt that a great many of the horses suffering from " cloudy eye " and imperfect vision is caused by dark stables and also white walls before their heads. Horses kept in a dark stable, and brought suddenly to the light, will wink their eyes and look about with a startled expression, being unable to distinguish the surrounding objects. Dealers will keep horses dark to make them look spirited when brought out for sale, often sowing the germs of disease, which will end either in partial or total blindness.

VENTILATION.

Upon this subject reason and common sense teach us that without fresh air nothing in animal or vegetable life can be healthy. Place a plant in a hot room without plenty of fresh air, and see how soon the most robust plant becomes sickly and pale. Then what can we think of those who keep such a valuable animal as the horse in a stable where the air is so bad that it would kill the vilest weed that grows upon mother earth ? Yet such is the ignorance displayed by the builder, that little or no ventilation is found in nearly all stables, and where there is any ventilation the prejudice of the groom often neutralises their best intentions. No horse should have less than 10,000 cubic feet of air to consume every hour of his life; then how is it possible for them to keep healthy if they do not get 1000 feet of air, let alone 10,000 feet per hour ? It is a well-known fact that after air has once passed through the lungs of man or beast, it is of no use to support life until it is again charged with oxygen from the surrounding atmosphere ; yet some grooms are so short-sighted that they will even stop the keyhole to exclude the air. I have seen stables in Leicestershire and also in Newmarket, which when opened on a frosty morning, the hot impure air would rush out so that anyone might suppose the stable to be on fire. The true principle of ventilation is to obtain a constant supply of fresh air without causing draught. This should be accomplished by grates on the outside of the stable through the wall, and brought up under the floor into the stable, which should have a double grate, the under portion made to slide, so as entirely to stop the upper space through the bars of the grate ; this would bring a supply of cold air upon the floor of the stable through the foundation of the walls. The hot air should be carried off through large grates up in the ceiling to allow the hot or consumed air to escape. These should be connected with air shafts, which should go through the roof. I don't mean those stove pipes so commonly used, which are not more than six inches in diameter, but shafts at least two feet square to carry off the foul air and ammonia that constantly arises in the stable. I have seen some of the stables which were possessed of these blessings, made into dens as foul as it is possible to conceive, by the ignorance of grooms who had charge of them, keeping the air passages entirely stopped with hay or other litter to keep the stable hot, to make the horse's coat shine like silk and lay close, not thinking that the same animal had to go out of his hot stable on a cold wet day, and perhaps stand in the wet and cold at a covert side for an hour at a stretch, shivering like a dog in a wet sack; and the moment the cold air caught the horse his coat would be up on end, and looking like a monster porcupine. It is an easy thing for a man to put on a great coat on a cold day; then, if the weather is cold, why not put extra clothing on the horse to keep him warm? Never resort to the false economy of keeping the stable hot at the expense of the health of your animal, or you will find yourself in the position of many grooms, who have their horses always delicate feeders, and for ever coughing with any change of the wind. Then they commence to put their arms down their horse's throat every morning to give him a cough ball, made of linseed meal and treacle, and enough nitre and camphor to make a taste and smell, and possessing the same virtues as the old woman's bread pills, which she warranted to do neither good or harm.

I went to look over some stables not 100 miles from

Hitchin, which their owner considered a marvel of perfection. He had no doubt spent a large amount upon
them, and I am sure I never saw a more miserable
failure. The stables were lofty, with traps into the
small roof to let the hot air out, but the roof was 14
inches thick of thatch, and no air shaft to convey the foul
air through the roof, consequently the air got in through
the false roof, and no further. The architect had
forgotten that pure air was required in the winter as
well as the summer, and there was no way of obtaining
it, only through the windows, which were high up, and
very small, close under the roof, giving no light into the
stable, and if they were open, threw a draught upon the
horses' backs. The doors were upon the sliding principle, and when closed I could put my fingers between
the door and the door-post, making the draught enough
to turn a mill. The groom told me that when he went
into the stable the first thing in the morning the ammonia was so strong that it brought tears from his eyes,
and almost choked him. This was called a first-class
stable—what a third-class one built by the same architect
and superintendent would be like I cannot guess. A
cold stable is not necessarily an unhealthy one, but it
is much better for the doors to be wide open than to fit
badly and cause great draught. Captain Hunt, who
used to keep a stud of horses at Great Bowden, near
Market Harborough, some years ago, always had his
stable doors wide open all weathers, and I never saw
horses look better in the field. His horses never caught
colds. Paddy Marr, a well-known groom of the old
school, used to take his horse to the river to drink every

morning, and he was about the only man in Melton Mowbray who escaped the influenza in 1837. Although I contend that a cold stable, under proper management, need not be an unhealthy one, yet I have a great horror of a damp and draughty stable. How few gentlemen, grooms, and architects, think anything about the dampness of stables, and make no convenience for washing horses, but have the horses washed in the stall or box they sleep in ; then, after saturating the bricks with water, the horse, after the fatigue of a hard day's work, has to lie upon a damp, cold bed, while the pores of his skin are relaxed by exertion. Next day he is stiff and sore, and in a day or two he commences to cough ; the groom is then blamed for the horse having caught cold. The evil effects of cold, damp, and ill-ventilated stables are well known to veterinary surgeons, from the number of horses suffering from rheumatism. I was once shown a valuable animal by Mr. Broad, M.R.C.V.S., of Star-street, Edgware-road, London, which was bought from a gentleman three days previous for £250. It was brought from his warm, dry stable, and put into a very damp one, and on the following morning it was unable to move ; the damp (it being of a delicate constitution) had struck to the bone, producing a violent attack of rheumatism, so bad, indeed, that upon passing the finger down the limbs, it produced a sound like the crackling of parchment. I have now endeavoured to show a few of the faults of the stable itself; in my next I will try to show what a stable ought to be. I am dealing with facts, and I am compelled to blame if I speak truthfully ; but I hope my readers will forgive me if my doctrine is not altogether pleasant, my object being to benefit both man and horse, being always proud to praise, yet not afraid to blame. I shall continue from time to time to praise or blame, according as the subject I treat deserves.

Having endeavoured to show a few faults of the stable, I will try and show what a stable should be to be healthy. The three most essential things required for the comfort of the horse are a dry, well-made and drained floor, large windows, and free ventilation. The floor of the stable should be paved with hard brick, laid upon a bed of concrete six inches thick. The brick should be laid dry, and afterwards soaked with clean water, then grouted with Portland cement; this will effectually prevent damp rising, and also prevent the urine from soaking through. The gutters, down the centre of the stall, should be shallow and running towards the fore feet, and the grate should be sunk half-an-inch lower than the bricks to allow for wear. Many floors are laid with the bricks level with the grate, and in a short time the bricks wear away, leaving a hollow alongside the grate where the urine will stand, and, the bricks getting saturated, become comparatively so many lumps of ammonia, poisoning the air with its fumes. The drains of all stables should be large, and of glazed tiles, and should have a fall of at least one inch in 40, to prevent accumulation of the small particles and the choking of the drains. The drains should run into a cesspool, so that the liquid manure may be saved if wanted for the garden; and what gardener will not want liquid manure if he can get it handy? The windows should be large, extending from near the roof

to within two feet of the ground, and should be moveable
from top and bottom. The stall should be six feet six
inches wide, and nine feet long, the manger should be
nine inches deep. I prefer Carson's iron mangers, with
water and hay crib. I do not like hay racks, as they
cause a waste of hay ; another great evil is, the horse is
apt to get hay-seed into his eyes, and cause violent
inflammation. A gentleman, some years ago, came to
me and told me his coachman had struck his horse over
the eye and nearly blinded him. He was in a great
rage, and said the fellow had had the impudence to tell
him he had never touched it, and he had discharged
him. He asked me to come and look at it for him, and
advise what should be done. I went with him, thinking
there must be some mistake, as I had known his coachman for some years as a kind, good-tempered man with
horses. When I reached the stables I had the horse
brought out to the light, and with the aid of a bodkin
threw back the eyelid, and exposed to the view of the
gentleman a hay-seed firmly embedded in the eye, and
it was with great difficulty that I removed it. It was a
seed of the Bearded Darnell (*Lolium Temulem*). The
explanation was sufficient, the gentlaman apologised,
and went away a wiser man. The stall should be high
enough to prevent the horses from getting their heads
over, so that they cannot bite each other in play. The
loose box should be at least 12 feet square. I hate
small boxes, for if a horse rolls he cannot roll over without getting cast. The ventilation should be as I
described in my last ; the ceiling should be at least 12
feet high, without lofts above the stables, but where they

are compelled to be for the value of space as in towns,
air-shafts should be carried from the stables through the
roof, and all communication from the stable shut off
by doors, as nothing spoils hay sooner than the smells
from a stable. A box or stall should be always made at
one end of the stable for the purpose of washing horses
after a journey, so that the floor of the stable can be
kept dry, The saddle-room should be in direct communication with the stable, as nothing is so bad for men
as to have to run out of doors in all weathers for everything they require. Many stablemen come to a pre-
mature grave by running out of a hot stable in their
shirtsleeves when in a state of perspiration; the cold
striking them, they become affected with asthma,
bronchitis, and rheumatism; yet not one stable in a
hundred has any regard paid to the comfort of the men.
The internal fittings of the stable are a matter of taste;
and as every crow thinks its own bird the whitest, so
every gentleman thinks his own stable the best. Having
tried to show what a stable ought and ought not to be,
I will proceed to the management of the horse in the
stable, and hope to be able to show that it is by kindness alone that we must resort to make the horse love,
fear, and obey. God, in his infinite wisdom, has formed
the horse so that it can be operated upon by the knowledge of man according to the dictates of his will, and
he might well be termed an unconscious, submissive
servant. This truth we see verified in every day's
experience by the abuses practised upon him. That he
is so constituted by nature that he will not offer resistance to any demand made of him which he fully

comprehends, if it is made in a way consistent with the laws of his nature. The horse, though possessed of some faculties superior to man, being devoid of reasoning powers, has no knowledge of right or wrong, and well it is so, for if he had sense equal to his strength, he would be useless to man. He would then demand the green fields for his inheritance, where he could roam at his pleasure, denying the right of servitude at all. To make him fit for the requirements of man, the colt has to be taught, and it is this teaching in its infancy that makes it a willing and useful servant, or spoils it altogether, by making it a vicious, worthless brute. No horse was ever born vicious ; it is not in his nature, and if he ultimately becomes so, it is the result of bad management. The teaching of a colt should commence at its mother's side, by the attendant constantly caressing it, and passing his hands gently down its legs and over its body, using kind words to it at the time.

The colt should never be entrusted to boys or thoughtless men, for they are sure to play with him, and it is this that ultimately makes the colt become a vicious horse. Hundreds of horses are spoiled in this manner. The colt is teased until he either kicks or bites his tormentor, then he is unmercifully beaten, and ever after it looks upon man as its natural enemy. As a proof that the horse is not naturally vicious, we find the most docile of animals the progeny of vicious sires. As an instance, Chanticleer was the most vicious horse of the present century, and he was made so by the man who looked after him tickling and pinching his flanks. So vicious was he, that for the last 15 years of his life he never had the bit out of his mouth, to which was attached a long chain; his mane and tail were never combed, and no blacksmith could touch his feet, and when he died, his hoofs had grown to nearly twelve inches long. Mr. Kime Hunter, of Thorpe Arnold, near Melton Mowbray, many years ago, owned a horse called Jingle Pot; he was very vicious, yet all his stock turned out quiet and docile. It is the most intelligent colt that becomes by mismanagement and bad treatment the vicious horse, hence the necessity of the utmost caution on the part of owners of young stock to obtain intelligent men to look after them. The training of the colt is a work that requires great pains, care, and patience, therefore it should not be entrusted to unskilful hands, which is too often the case. Many valuable animals are totally spoiled by the ignorance displayed by their trainers, who often have no patience and as little judgment; therefore they expect the colt to do things which they have not the sense to teach it, and then ill-use it because it does not understand. Such men should be placed in a foreign country among men whose language they cannot understand to be their taskmasters, who should punish them every time they make a mistake, then they perhaps would have more patience with the poor animal under their care, and not expect it to do things until it has been taught what it is expected to do. The careful trainer will commence with the colt at its mother's side. By carefully handling it, he will teach it to hold up its legs by lifting gently at the fetlock, and always using the words "hold up." The colt soon recognises the sound, and as it finds it is not hurt, it becomes more willing, and at last will hold up its foot with telling. The trainer should on no account strike a colt, as every lesson it has to learn can be taught by kind and gentle treatment. After the colt is taken from its mother, it should be gently handled; first, get a soft webb headcollar, such as are supplied by Messrs. Black-well, the celebrated saddlers of Oxford-street, and use the colt to be led about, but do not use it to be led always on the near side, a fault too common, but teach it to be led on both near and off side. Should it show any signs of play, one cross word will be all the remonstrance that will be required to check it. Such is its timid nature, that if it jumps or kicks, you speak sternly to it, it will tremble at your voice. The old proverb says, " Man is what a woman makes him," and the horse is what the man makes him, either kind, gentle, loving, affectionate, or revengeful and savage. All horses have good memories, and recollect those who have been kind or unkind to them.

Having thoroughly learned your colt to be led, the next lesson you have to teach is to allow the bit to be put into its mouth. This is rather a difficult task to accom-plish; first use the colt to allow you to put your fingers into its mouth, then hold its head, gently but firmly, with the right hand while you place the bit between its teeth with your left. The bit should never be allowed to remain on the colt more than half-an-hour above time. By keeping it on longer you weary your colt, and it becomes sulky. No lesson should be of long duration, but often repeated, and the bit should be large and plain. Never use a sharp bit on a colt, as it makes the mouth sore, and when once a colt has a sore mouth it is sure to become hard-mouthed. When you have accomplished bitting and leading the colt, you next prepare a caversoon and lounging rein. Make sure it will fit the colt without hurting it, as this is a powerful apparatus intended to confine the nose. This should be used very gently, as instances have been known of the bones and gristle of the nose becoming diseased from harshly pulling the caversoon. It must now be led round a ring on soft ground, and taught to walk and trot both ways and round also. Caress it whenever it does right, and do not let it run round the circle too long, as it produces giddiness. We next use it to the roller, and afterwards to the dumb jockey. Thanks to Mr. Blackwell, the old clumsy wooden jockey has become a thing of the past, and his whalebone and gutta-percha jockey, with their indiarubber reins, have done away with the cruel unyielding side rein. These jockeys are admirably adapted to teach the colt to bend its head, and at the same time to insure the colt having a light even mouth. When the colt has become tractable to all its lessons, loose straps may be hung upon the jockey to accustom it to the flapping of various parts of its harness, and prevent it becoming restive. A few days will suffice to teach it all it is required, and make it endure it patiently, for as it finds that it is not hurt by them, it soon becomes reconciled to them, and the more gentle and kind we are the less trouble they give, for as they gain confidence in us the more they will let us do to them, Powell, in his work, published in the beginning of this century, gives us the following as his system of approaching a colt. I record it here, as it may be useful to those

B

of my readers who have wild colts; but I contend that we ought not to have wild colts to tame if we use them right in their infancy. He says "A horse is gentled by my secret in from four to sixteen hours," the time I have most commonly employed is from four to six hours. He goes on to say, "Cause your horse to be put into a small yard or stable; if in a stable it ought to be large to give him exercise with the halter before you lead him out. If the horse belongs to that class which appears only to fear man, you must introduce yourself gently into the stable or yard where he is. He will naturally run away from you, and frequently turn his head from you, but you must walk about extremely soft and slow, so that he can see you whenever he turns his head towards you, which he never fails to do in a quarter of an hour, or half hour at most. I never knew one much longer without turning his head toward me. At the very moment he turns his head hold out your left hand towards him and stand perfectly still, keeping your eyes upon the horse, watching his motions, if he makes any; if the horse does not stir from ten to fifteen minutes, advance as slowly as possible without any other ingredients in your hand than what nature puts in it." He says I have made use of certain ingredients before people, such as the sweat under my arm, to disguise the real secret, and many believed that the docility to which the horse arrived in so short a time was owing to these ingredients. But you see from this explanation that they were of no use whatever. The implicit faith placed in these ingredients, though innocent of themselves, become faith without works, and thus men remain always in doubt concerning the secret. If the

horse makes the least motion when you advance towards
him stop and remain perfectly still until he is quiet.
Remain in this condition a few minutes and then advance
again in the same slow and almost imperceptible manner,
and take notice if the horse stirs to stop without changing your position. It is very uncommon for a horse to
stir more than once, he generally keeps his eye steadfast
upon you until you are near enough to touch him on
his forehead. When you are thus near to him raise
slowly and by degrees your hand, and let it come in
contact with that part just above the nostrils as lightly
as possible. If the horse flinches (as many will) repeat
with great rapidity these light strokes upon his forehead,
going a little further up towards his ears by degrees and
descend with the same rapidity until he will let you
handle his forehead all over, when the strokes can be repeated with more force, descending by lighter strokes to
each side of his head, until you can handle that part with
equal facility. Then touch in the same light manner,
making your hands and fingers play around the lower
part of the horse's ears, coming down now and then to
his forehead, which may be looked upon as the helm that
governs all the rest. Having succeeded in handling his
ears advance towards his neck with the same precautions
and in the same manner, observing always to augment
the force of the stroke whenever the horse will permit it;
perform the same on both sides of the neck until he lets
you take it in your arms without flinching. Proceed in
the same progressive manner to the sides and then to the
back of the horse ; every time the horse shows nervousness
return immediately to the forehead, as the true standard,

patting him with your hands, and thence rapidly to where you had already arrived, always gaining ground a considerable distance farther every time this happens; the head, ears, neck and body being tenderest, proceed from the back to the root of the tail.

This must be managed with great dexterity as a horse is never to be depended on that is skittish about the tail. Let your hands fall lightly and rapidly on that part next to the body a minute or two, and then you will begin to give it a slight pull every quarter of a minute, at the same time you continue this augment the force of the strokes, as well as the raising of the tail, until you can raise it with the greatest of ease, which generally happens in a quarter of an hour in most horses, and in others almost immediately. It remains now to handle all his legs; from the tail come back again to the head, handle it well, also the ears, breast, neck, &c., speaking now and then to the horse. Begin by degrees to descend to the legs, always ascending and descending, gaining ground every time you descend until you get to its feet. Talk to the horse in Latin, Greek, French, English, or Spanish, or in any other language you please, but let him hear the sound of your voice, which at the beginning is not quite necessary, but which I have always done in making it lift up its feet. At the time of speaking to it lift its foot with your hand. It soon becomes familiar with sounds and will hold up its feet, and in a short time the horse will let you lift them and even take them up in your arms. All this operation is no magnetism, no galvanism; it is merely taking away the fear a horse generally has of man, and familiarising the animal with his master. As the horse doubtless experiences a certain amount of pleasure from this handling he will soon become gentle under it, and show a very marked attachment to his keeper. Rarey, in his treatment of horses, says "The horse that has only a natural fear of man is the easiest trained, for when we have that which is wild and lively we can train him to our will in a very short time, as they are generally quiet to obey." There is another kind that are of a stubborn or vicious disposition, and although they are not wild and do not require taming in the sense it is generally understood, they are just as ignorant as the wild horse, if not more so, and need to be taught as much. In order to have them obey quickly, it is necessary that they should be made to fear their master, as in order to obtain perfect obedience from any horse we must first have him to fear us ; our motto is "Fear, love, and obey," and we must have the fulfilment of the two first before we can expect the latter. It is by our philosophy of creating fear, love, and confidence, that we govern to our will every kind of horse. Then, in order to take horses as we find them, of all kinds, and train them to our liking, we always take with us, when we go into the stable to a colt, a long switch whip (whalebone buggy whips are the best) with a good silk cracker so as to cut keenly and make a sharp report, accompanied with a sharp fierce word, will be sufficient to enliven the spirits of any horse. With this whip in your right hand, the lash pointing backward, enter the stable alone, as it is a great disadvantage in training horses to have anyone in the stable with you, so that nothing should attract the colt's attention. If it is wild, you will soon see it on the opposite side of the stable to you, and then is the time to use a little judgment. I should not want myself more than three-quarters of an hour to handle any kind of colt, and have him running about in the stable after me. I would advise a new beginner to take more time and not to hurry; if there is but one colt, and it is not particular what time you expend, and have not had experience in handling colts, I would advise such to take Mr Powell's method, which he says takes from four to six hours. But, as I want to accomplish the same, and teach him to be led in less than one hour, I shall give you a much quicker process of accomplishing the same end. When you have entered the stable, stand still, and let the horse look at you for a minute or two, and as soon as he is settled in one position, approach him slowly with both arms stationary, your right hand hanging by your side, holding the whip as directed, the left bent at the elbow with the hand projecting. As you approach it, go not too near to its head or its croup, so as not to make it move either forward or backward. Step a little to the right or left cautiously; this will keep it in one place. As you get very near draw a little to his shoulder and stop a few seconds; if you are within reach it will turn its head and smell your hand. As soon as it touches its nose to your hand caress it as before directed, always using a very light soft touch, always rubbing the same way the hair lies, so that your hand will pass along as smoothly as possible. As you stand by its side you may find it more convenient to rub its neck or the side of its head, which will answer the same purpose as rubbing its forehead. Favour every inclination of the horse to smell or touch you with his nose, always following each touch or communication of this kind with the most tender and affectionate caresses, accompanied with a kind look and pleasant word of some sort, constantly repeating the same words, with the same kind, steady, tone of voice, as the horse soon learns to read the expression of the face and voice, and will know as well when fear, love, or anger prevails, as you know your own feelings. Rarey's mode of treatment if the horse is of a stubborn disposition :—

" If your horse instead of being wild seems to be of a stubborn or mulish disposition, if he lays back his ears as you approach him or turns his heels to kick you, he has not that regard or fear of man that he should have to enable you to handle him quickly and easily, and it might be well to give him a few sharp cuts with the whip against the legs close to the body. It will crack keenly as it plies round the legs, and the crack of the whip will affect him more than two or three over the back, the skin on the inner part of the legs or about the flank, being thinner and more tender than on his back. Do not whip him much—just enough to scare him. It is not because we want to hurt the horse that we whip him ; we only do it to scare the bad disposition out of him ; but whatever is done, do quickly, sharply, and with fire ; but without anger. If you are going to scare him at all, you must do it at once ; never go into a pitch battle with your horse and whip him until he is mad and will fight you ; you had better not touch him at all, for you will establish, instead of fear and regard, feelings of resentment,

hatred, and ill-will. It will do him no good to strike
a blow, unless you can scare him, but if you can succeed
in scaring him, you can whip him without making
him mad. Fear and anger never exist together in the
horse, and as soon as one is visible, you find the other
has disappeared. As soon as you have frightened him
so that he will stand up straight, and pay some attention to you, approach him again and caress him a great
deal more than you whipped him, then you will excite
the two controlling passions of his nature—love and
fear—and he will love and fear you too, and, as soon
as he learns what to do, will obey quickly." Although
I have given at some length Powell's and Rarey's
systems of training wild horses, yet in a country like
England there ought not to be wild horses to tame.
The Arabians manage their young horses much better
than we do. They having no other house but a tent
to live in; this also serves them for a stable, so that
the mare, foal, husband, wife, and children, lie all
together indiscriminately. The little children are often
seen upon the body or neck of the mare, which continues inoffensive and harmless, permitting them to
play and caress it without injury. They never beat
their horses, but treat them gently; they speak to
them and seem to hold discourse with them. They
use them as friends. They never try to increase
speed with whip or spur, unless in a case of great
necessity; however, when this happens they set off
with amazing swiftness, and leap over obstacles with
the agility of a buck, and if their rider happens to fall,
they are so manageable that they stand still in the

midst of their most rapid career. So gentle and docile are they that it is a common sight to see the Bedouin children playing under the belly of their horse or climbing up its legs. The foal being used from its birth to gentle treatment and caressing, looks upon man as his best friend, and as it grows it develops a steadfast love for him. How different the treatment it receives in this boasted Christian land.

Having taught the colt to bear the jockey, next place the saddle on its back. Be careful not to frighten it and go up to it very gently with the saddle under your right arm, having the girths folded over the saddle, and your hand holding the off-side flap. Get close to your colt and raise the arm slowly and then bring the saddle over its back and lay it softly on it. After the saddle is on its back, keep playing with it, and let the girths fall over, then buckle the girth but not tight. After you have got the saddle on take two lounging reins, one on each side, and drive it about, stopping it occasionally to pat and talk to it. It should be driven about for a few days, and then you may get on its back. This you should always do in the stable, getting up and down very quietly, speaking kindly, and patting and caressing it. As it is wonderful how a horse can read man's countenance, and tell instantly the mood a man is in ; therefore it is necessary that the man training a young horse should not lose his temper.

After you have mounted and dismounted several times and walked it round the box, to accustom the colt to the use of the reins, you can take it out and teach it to walk. I once heard a gentleman say, "Any fool can make a horse go fast," and it is quite true; therefore it is equally true that it requires skill and patience to teach a horse its slow paces, which adds much to the value of a horse. Many horses can trot and gallop fast, but cannot walk, and are miserable brutes to ride. Therefore teach your horse to walk, and when it can walk well it will be time enough to make it trot. Teach it all its paces distinct, as nothing is so bad as to have a horse that will neither walk, trot, canter, nor gallop, but wants to mix all its paces into one. When you ride the colt, which should be done half-an-hour at a time twice each day, do not let anyone touch the bridle while you mount. If it is necessary for an attendant to hold the colt while you mount, let him place his hand gently on its nose, and stroke its head. Always make the colt stand still after you are on its back for a few seconds, and in the same manner make it stand still before you dismount. After you have used it to this treatment for a week or two, it will stand perfectly still for you to either mount or dismount. As the horse, through life, is required to do all kinds of things, it is necessary that it should be taught in its youth to do what it may in after-life be called upon to perform. We have now taught the colt to carry man, and walk, trot, or canter at his will; we will now use it to the sword and fire-arms. Having buckled your scabbard on without the sword, go to its head, caress it, and let it examine the scabbard before you mount; then, after it is satisfied, mount and walk slowly, to let it feel the scabbard; after it is

used to it you can unloop the scabbard and let it have
full play.   In a day or two it will make no objection to
carry it, when you can put the sword in, and use it to
be quietly drawn and replaced, and in a short time
with kind words and gentle usage you can draw the
sword with a sharp ring and it will take no notice.
Next you can proceed to wave the sword above its
head, and to cut, parry, and point, without your horse
moving a leg or ear.   If you are rough and harsh with
the colt, you cannot teach it as much in a month as a
kind man can in three days.   Our horse now knows
that the sword is not meant to hurt it, so we will now
use the pistol.   We first accustom it to seeing us hold
out the pistol at arm's length, then we snap a cap.   He
will start and prick his ears, and kind reassuring words
are now wanted.   When you have quieted him, snap
another cap, and he will start again, but will not take
so much notice as at first, and in a short time you can
snap as many caps as you like without it taking any
notice.   You must now place a very small quantity
of gunpowder in the pistol, to make a report a little
louder than the cap and cause a little smoke, and as your
colt gets used to the report you can increase it until you
get a full charge.   When it will stand the use of the
pistol, you can then use the carbine, and the colt will
be now made a broken charger.   We will next put it
into harness.   It may not be required for harness, but
like man it cannot learn too much.   Many horses are put
into harness before they are half broken to the saddle,
their owners being impatient, and often so parsimonious
that they will not allow the breaker time to teach the

colt, therefore the colt leaves the breaker's hands raw and half broken, and goes into inexperienced hands, and the breaker gets the credit of the colt being practically useless.   If they come to grief they conveniently throw all the blame upon the man who would have broken it thoroughly and turned it out a useful, docile animal had he had time allowed him.   Although men have written works out of number upon the breaking and training of horses from the time of Marcus Paulus (who tells us he saw in Persia studs of ten thousand white mares all together, and very fleet) to the present time, yet none of the theories advanced can always be put in practice, and although some writers claim to tame or break a horse in a few hours and others a few days, yet I never saw a horse that was made perfect in the saddle or harness without much time, pains, and patience being bestowed upon it. Any colt-breaker who trains a colt, to make it perfect in its paces, quiet in harness, stand the use of fire-arms, and carry accoutrements, loses no time if he does it in a month.   Owners of horses would find themselves much better off, and have more useful and valuable animals if they allowed the trainer more time, although it cost a pound or two more.   After the colt has been used to the saddle and dumb-jockey we proceed to put the harness upon it.   This, as in all other lessons the colt has to learn, should be done with gentleness, speaking kindly and always caressing.   When you have succeeded in putting the harness on, lead it about for a day or two, then put long reins on and proceed to drive it along the road, use it to pass stone-heaps, clothes upon the hedges, traction engines, or anything that is likely to make it shy.   When you have driven it for a few days, teach it by gently pulling both reins to back, always saying some kind word to it, and in a short time the horse will understand what is wanted of it, and will answer the bit instantly. After it is used to being driven, put long traces on; the horse will not mind them if you have used it to the reins touching its legs when driving it. You now get a log of wood, an old gatepost will do, drive in two staples about four feet apart, and attach your traces to the log. The traces should be quite as long as leading traces for tandem. You now drive the horse, with the log attached, round a field. After the horse will draw it quietly, take it on the road to let it hear the noise; it will not require to be driven with the log more than three times before you can put it with safety into the break alongside an old quiet horse. After it has been driven both sides in double harness, it may be put in single harness and carefully driven, but should not be driven far, one mile out and back is quite sufficient at one time. After the colt has been in harness and brought back to the stable, its shoulders should be bathed with strong salt and water to prevent them getting tender. More horses are made jibbers by the shoulder being allowed to become tender than anything else. Having given a brief outline of the colt, I will now proceed to the management of it in the stable, and upon this subject the well-being of the horse depends, as the horse requires light and ventilation in its stable, so it requires food and attention from the groom. Feeding is the most important part of stable management, yet how few use any discretion in this matter, but feed horses at any time and in any quantity, knowing or caring little whether they injure the horse or not. The old proverb says, " Full feed, then rest, often feed does best," and in this case it is strictly true. It would seem that nature had wisely foreseen that the horse was destined to become the servant of man, and to render it more valuable and fitted to the labour that would be required of it, it became necessary to diminish the inconvenience and danger which would necessarily accompany a large stomach, and so ordained that the animal should have one proportioned to the position it was destined to fill in creation. The great bulk of its frame requires a large amount of food to be consumed to afford nutriment, yet the stomach is wisely formed small to prevent pressure as much as possible, and in addition it has the power to rapidly decompose the food, which speedily descends to a portion ot the intestines remote from the diaphragm, where the pressure of food cannot inconvenience it. Indeed, the whole of its food is very quickly digested, and very soon passed through, otherwise it could not be sustained in strength. Considering the small amount ot nutriment contained in the common food of the horse, hence the force ot the proverb, and the stupidity of those grooms who neglect to feed the horse often and at regular intervals. In this we also see the wise and far-seeing handiwork ot the Creator, for the horse, unlike the ox, has no gaul-bladder, to let at intervals a quantity of bile into the stomach to aid its digestion, but the bile is carried through the liver direct to the *duodenum* or first gut, so that it is always supplied with the necessary bile to promote a rapid digestion. No horse ought to be fed less than four times each day, neither ought it to have violent exercise directly after feeding. Indeed, it is a safe maxim to always go the first and last mile of a journey slow. The horse should always have water before his food; if you give it water after its food, it being drunk rapidly, will carry the food through the stomach in an undigested state and be likely to cause obstruction of the bowels, the food not being deprived of its acids, which would be carried into the blood to support life. There are many stud-grooms who will neither water nor feed their horse before going out for a day's hunting; others will give a little corn and no water, and think the horse can go twelve or fourteen miles to cover, and perhaps gallop thirty or forty miles in the course of the day upon an empty stomach, when its entire digestive system is so quick that the food is consumed in half-an-hour. Then it has to work often from twelve to eighteen hours without food or water.

The grooms then wonder how the horse's digestive system goes wrong. First it is smothered in a hot, unhealthy, ill-ventilated stable; then it is either burst with food or starved. Sometimes the blame does not lie at the door of the groom, but with the master, who thinks he knows all about horses, because he buys them, and will not allow a groom to use his own discretion, and is afterwards grieved to find that his horses are unable to carry him through a hard run. That a horse can run well after being well fed has often been proved. When a boy, a friend of mine, a stud-groom now in Leicestershire, went to Ireland for Punchestown races with a horse called Oakstick. The night before the race the lad had to sleep in the loose box with the horse, which was tied up, but during the night it managed to slip its headcollar. The lad had brought a bushel of corn with him, and at night brought a pail of water into the stable for the morning's use, and being very tired lay down upon a sack and fell asleep; the horse being awake and loose, amused itself by eating nearly all the corn and drinking all the water. When the lad awoke at about four o'clock in the morning the old horse was blown out like a barrel. The lad was in a sad way, and hardly knew what to do; however, he took the horse out and walked it about for two or three hours, then brought him into the stable and put a muzzle on him. He was afraid to tell the trainer what had happened, and at two o'clock the horse was taken to the saddling paddock, the flag fell, and Oakstick sailed away, never running better in his life, and won the race (a four mile steeplechase) in a common canter against sixteen others. Neither of us have ever sent our horses out for a hard day's work hungry since. I know one gentleman now who will not allow his groom to feed his horse more than twice a-day, and he is surprised to find that it suffers from indigestion. After letting the heat of its stomach consume itself for ten hours per day, and when the horse is famishing with hunger, giving it as much as it can consume, it does not properly chew its food, but it swallows it whole. I was once asked by a gentleman how I managed with a bad-feeding horse, to which I replied that I never had one many days. But, said the gentleman, if you had one would you not give tonic powders. I replied, certainly, such as nature supplies. " What do you mean ? " he asked. I said, "If I

have a horse off its feed because its digestive organs are up-
set, I take it out in the fresh air for half-an-hour in the
morning before feeding. After it has had its walk, I bring
it in and let it drink what cold water it likes, and then give
it a small quantity of corn and a little sweet hay. I give
little at one time, but feed often, and in a few days, without the aid of any drugs, I find my horse always ready for
his food." No horse gets less medicine than the horse of
a veterinary surgeon, and I believe with Shakespeare,
" Throw physic to the dogs ;" yet it is necessary for every
groom with horses under his care to have a knowledge of
the drugs commonly used for the horse, and the effects it
produces. No man uses less drugs than the man who
thoroughly understands them. It is the abuse of drugs,
not the use of them, that has to be deprecated. If a groom
has a knowledge of drugs, he is of great use to the
veterinary surgeon, for he will watch minutely the effects
of medicine left to be given to the patient, and will be
able to inform the practical veterinary surgeon the symptoms that have taken place since his last visit. The
veterinary surgeon has great drawbacks to contend with
in the treatment of animals, and I am afraid he has too
often reason to find fault with the ignorance of the groom.
This is not to be wondered at, as a great many gentlemen
take lads from the plough, and in a few years, without
any training, and without any knowledge of the business
beyond cleaning a set of harness, washing a carriage, and
dressing a dirty horse, he is put into the position of groom
or coachman, and the trust and care of valuable animals
thrust upon him. It is this sort of thing that makes the
name of a stableman the scoff of a large number of gentle-

C

men, and enables them to ride their hobby-horses and air them at almost every dinner-table, by a never-failing discourse about their fools of grooms, who have let their horses get the influenza, or have thrown their horses down and broken their knees. The groom always *throws* the horse down, the horse always *falls* down with the master. A gentleman once went to the late Mr. Field, veterinary surgeon, of Oxford-street, and told him his groom had thrown his horse down, and he had discharged him. Mr. Field asked, " Did your man throw it down ? " and was answered, " Yes, decidedly ; " to which Mr Field replied, " Then when you have done with your man have the kindness to send him to me ; I will find him employment; he will be very valuable to me, as I often want a horse thrown down, and have to employ five or six men to do it. As your man can throw a horse by himself, if I give him good wages, it will be a saving to me. I have no doubt, Captain, that if the horse had come down with you, you would have found a reason to account for it." The veterinary surgeon prescribes medicine for his patient, but he is not sure that the medicine is given at proper times, or even given at all. The chances are if the horse is at all awkward he never gets it at all, and another great danger is that the reasoning power of the groom who knows nothing about the effects of drugs will lead him to reason that if ten drops will do any good, forty drops must do four times as much, so down go four doses at once, and when the veterinary surgeon calls next day he either finds the horse dead or the symptoms greatly aggravated. Although, as a class, the groom is considered ignorant and illiterate, yet there are many intelligent men among them, men who have made the horse the study of their lifetime, therefore it is not fair or just to call all grooms fools. There is no doubt that if there were more facilities given to the groom to study, we should find many bright men amongst them. We send women to the hospitals to train for nurses, and find it a great success and an immense help to the surgeon. Yet more the pity that there is no class in the college of Veterinary Surgeons where the grooms could go through a course of nursing the sick and afflicted horse. A class of this sort would bring the intelligent men to the front; they could pass an examination, and receive a certificate qualifying them as fit to take charge of sick horses. The man holding such certificate would be of great value to the veterinary surgeon and gentlemen who employed them. They would not be the class of men whom we too often find in the position of coachmen and grooms, and, because they are ignorant, cause a stigma to be cast upon the whole fraternity. I am bound to say with Tom Hood, that "evil is wrought by want of thought as much as want of heart." How often do we hear gentlemen and grooms asking each other if their horses cough. It is a very rare occurrence that I have to answer "Yes," yet there are times when both man and horse take cold without any given cause, but they are very rare occurrences. Then you may well ask, "How do horses catch cold?" Some will tell us, by standing about in the cold, which in some cases is true, and it is wonderful that a great many more horses do not catch cold when we see grooms out under the pretence of exercising, but in reality going from one public-house to another drinking, and when they come home they leave their horses wet and dirty while they are drinking there little sense away at a public-house bar. There is another cause of the horse catching cold and coughing, and this is to be seen every day at Newmarket—that place where they think they cannot be taught anything, and that to them everything is but a tale already told. The great cause of cold-catching is not, as most people suppose, by going out of a warm stable into the cold, but by coming direct from the cold into the hot air of the stable, and causing a too sudden relaxing of the pores of the skin, making the skin too sensitive, when the least draught causes a check and chill, and the animal soon commences to cough. As I have before stated, after washing the horse in the stall or box he has to sleep in, the damp of the floor rises and penetrates the skin, which produces influenza (by depriving it of animal electricity), the worst complaint the horse is subject to, a short history of which will not be out of place here.

Influenza is no new complaint; it was well known to our forefathers. There is very little doubt but it was known to the Romans, and was called the plague. We have authentic accounts of influenza from Solleysel, a celebrated veterinary surgeon of the German army, in the year 1648. It began by fever, great prostration, tears running from the eyes, and an abundant mucous discharge of a greenish colour from the nostrils. The horses experienced loss of appetite and the ears were cold, and few of those attacked recovered. The treatment adopted was with a view to neutralise the malignity of the poison and to fortify nature, for it was a poison, says this writer, which gave rise to the disorder and was the cause of fever. Precautions were taken to have all the healthy horses removed from the infected stables, and they were not to return to them until they had been fumigated, whitewashed, and otherwise cleaned. Solleysel designated it a *fièvre pestilentrelle*, very deadly at its commencement, but afterwards amenable to medical treatment. A catarrhal fever had been epidemic the previous year. Again, the years 1688 and 1693 were marked by epidemic influenza and epizootic influenza. In 1712 the horses of Europe were again attacked with epizootic influenza, but the records collected are very imperfect. It was not until the year 1727 that the records notice the erratic or invasive character of the disease. This peculiarity is noticed in a chronological history of the weather and of the prevailing diseases of Dublin, by Mr John Kutty, M.D., London, 1770. He says, " In November in Staffordshire and Shropshire horses were suddenly seized with cough and weakness, disabling them from work. In December, both in Dublin and the remote parts of the kingdom, horses were seized with a cough and shortness of breath, and sometimes sore throat ; some bled at the nose, others had a large discharge of thick phlegm from the nose, which, being long-continued, was salutiferous; some died in the streets, partly through improper medicine. In 1732 influenza swept over Europe and North America ; its effect on mankind, and its progress from place to place, are fully and carefully recorded." It was also epizootic, as appears from the following extract from Medical Essays and Observations,

published in Edinburgh:—"We believe it will not be
improper here to mention that the horses in and about
this place are being universally attacked with a running
at the nose and cough, towards the end of October and the
middle of November, before the appearance of this fever
of cold among men." The epizootic of 1732 was observed
in London by William Gibson, author of a New Treatise
on the Diseases of the Horse, in 1754. In Gibson's
account we have as accurate a description of the events
of the year 1873 as of those occurring one hundred and
forty years before. About the end of the year 1732 there
was a remarkable distemper among horses in London
and in several other parts of the kingdom. They were
seized suddenly with a vehement dry, sounding cough,
which shook them so violently that some of them were
often ready to drop down with hard straining and want
of breath ; their throats were raw and sore, many of them
had their kernels (submaxillary glands) swollen, and
were painful to the touch. For the first two days most
of them refused all manner of food as well as water, and
had so many other bad signs that when this distemper
first broke out, many were afraid of a mortality among
them. Indeed, the only good sign they had was the
vehemence of their cough, that kept the blood in motion,
and speedily set their noses running, and which generally
began the third day, and continued in a profuse manner
for five or six days. Some of them in that time discharged as much as two or three pails would hold of
purulent matter, which, however, was of a laudable
colour and good consistence. While the running at
the nose continued they would not feed much, though

their appetites were craving, because the matter, mingled with their food, made it altogether disagreeable, so that they lost flesh exceedingly. This loss of flesh proved a benefit to them rather than a detriment, and as soon as the running abated they ate voraciously, and soon recovered their flesh. This distemper, though in noways mortal, yet was so very catching that when any horses were seized with it, I observed that those which stood on each side of it were generally infected as soon as it began to run at the nose. In the same manner the small-pox communicates the infection when it is upon the turn. While this lasted, above 100 troop horses under my care were seized with it. I always caused the sick horses to be removed from the healthy, as soon as they were taken ill, and put by themselves as in a hospital. In one troop of Horse Grenadiers, we filled a stable of thirty-six standings in three days, an infirmary of five standings, and another of eighteen, in three or four days more. Nevertheless all of them recovered in a short time. In 1743 the influenza prevailed as an epidemic in England, and a few doubtful words quoted both by Fleming and by Dr. Thompson seem to indicate an epizootic influenza among horses. In 1750 an epizootic passed through Great Britain and Denmark which resembled in all its features that of the epizootic in 1873. Kutty says, "About the middle or end of December the most epidemic and universally spreading disease among horses that any one living remembered made its appearance in Dublin, which seems to have been nearly analogous to the influenza and catarrhal fever which seized mankind in the years 1737 and 1743, but now particularly attacked the horses in their turn, as may appear by a comparison of their respective histories. It had appeared in England in November and spread through all England almost in an instant, and toward the end of the month began to abate. It raged in Denmark at the same time, but did not reach our horses in Dublin till its decline in England at the time before-mentioned. It affected the horses in Munster and Ulster almost if not quite as soon as in Dublin, and there was scarce an instance of a horse in the town or country but what had it. It seized the horses like a violent cold with heaviness, loss of appetite, cough, and laborious breathing, and then a profuse running at the nose and mouth of a digested or thick yellow-greenish matter, upon which they become better in England as well as here." In the epizootic of 1750 post-mortem appearances similar to those described in 1873 in the epizootic then raging, *purpura hemorrhagica,* were noted by an author named Osmore in " A Treatise on the Diseases and Lameness of Horses" (London, 1766). His words are, " On many of these I have made several incisions; I found in all of them a quantity of extravasated serum lodged between the skin and the membranes." In the year 1758 the influenza was both epidemic and epizootic in Great Britain. Dr. Robert Wytt, of Edinburgh, wrote—" A gentleman told me that in the Carse of Gowrie (a large valley in Perthshire) in the month of September, before this disease was perceived, the horses were more than usually affected with cold and cough." In regard to the same year, Fleming

writes—"Influenza appeared in Stirlingshire, in the
north of Scotland, in the months of September and
October, and horses seem to have been affected with
cold and cough at the outset of the attack on man.
Vast numbers of horses died during this year in London
and neighbourhood from an epizootic, probably influenza."
Two years later, in 1760, influenza was again epizootic
in Great Britain and other portions of Europe. Fleming,
referring to this year, writes—"At the same time an
epizootic manifested itself amongst horses, which affected, it is supposed, every animal in the locality "—
Cleveland, county of Cork. It was very fatal among
horses in London in January, as the chronicle of the
Annual Register for that month says—" A distemper
which rages amongst the horses makes great havoc in
and about towns. Nearly one hundred died in one
week. Ophthalmia prevailed during the north-east winds
of April, and an epizootic amongst horses at the same
time, of a nature of an epidemic catarrhal fever, which
took its rise in the winter, and was also common to
other parts of Europe. It raged in London and other
parts of England, in January, February, and March,
and seized our horses in Dublin at the end of March.
Moved westward as other epidemics frequently do,
and on the 4th of April it had become general in this
city, and continued to the end of that month. The
mules also were affected." The latter part of 1775,
was marked in England by an epidemic of influenza.
The historian of this epidemic, Dr Fothergill, of
London, with praiseworthy zeal, collected reports from
all his medical brethren in all parts of England who

were disposed to respond to his printed circulars calling for information. These reports are to be found in Dr. Thompson's annals of influenza. The disease prevailed from the middle of October to the middle of December, 1775, and it appears from the following extracts from the above-mentioned reports that influenza was epizootic among horses in the preceding August and September. Dr. Fothergill, writing in London, says, " During this time horses and dogs were much affected, those especially which were well kept. The horses had severe coughs, were hot, forbore eating, and were long in recovering." Dr. Williams, of Dorchester, writes, " After the middle of August I have heard from good authority that a disorder among horses prevailed very generally in Yorkshire." Dr. Thomas Glass, of Exeter, writes, " I have only to add that in these parts of the country, in the month of September, many horses and dogs were severely afflicted with colds and coughs." Dr. Haygarth, of Chester, writes, " About August and September, in North Wales, almost all the horses were seized with coughs." Dr. R. Pulteney, of Blamford, writes, " I heard much of horses and dogs being afflicted before we heard of it among the human race."

The following quotation from Fleming's work refers to the year 1782:—" An epizootic of influenza appears to have prevailed in Europe at the same time as the epidemic in man." Huveman observed and reported upon it as it manifested itself in Germany ; and Abilguard, the talented founder of the Veterinary School at Copenhagen, has left an admirable monograph of this disease, which he had ample time and opportunity of studying, during the period it affected the King of Denmark's stallions. This epizootic did not reach England, or if it did, we can find no record of it. For the year 1797 Fleming writes, " Influenza was very severe in New York and Philadelphia, and over a large tract of that Continent; at the same time there was a great mortality among the horses in Maryland." During the prevalence of epidemic influenza in 1803 all kinds of domestic animals seem to have been affected with unusual diseases, but it is impossible, in the annals of influenza (pp. 213—215) to find good evidence of epizootic influenza among horses. In Mr. Barlow's remarks occurs the following statement in regard to influenza among horses, " It reappeared again among horses very extensively and severely in 1815.' John Field, of London, records the remarkable prevalence of the disease in 1819 and 1823, since that time and up to the present, we find many records of its occurrence in the *Veterinarian.* It is singular that although of late years scarcely twelve consecutive months have passed without many cases being observed, yet at intervals of four years influenza seems to give us a specially severe visitation. Thus it is noticed by Wilkinson in 1815, by Field in 1819 and 1823, by Percival in 1828, 1832, 1840, and 1844. Many remember it in 1848 and still better in 1852. Thus, excepting an interval of five years from 1823 to 1828, we can trace its periods of aggravation in four-year circles from 1815 to the present time.

Having given the history of influenza at some length to show that it is no disease, I will now proceed to the cause, symptoms, and treatment of this malignant disease. Mr Thomas Greaves says in an admirable paper, written in the year 1865, "The pestilence that walked in darkness is no fiction. Both sacred and profane writers find ample proof that from the very earliest times down to the present age man has been periodically startled by its silent, invisible, but irresistible agency. Well might the ancients in their terror attribute it to the destroying angel. But its destructive influence has not been confined to man; animals have been from time to time swept off in multitudes. The cause or causes appeared at the time inscrutable; but in all probability they were one and the same agency, and their degree of virulence was dependent upon certain modified circumstances. Notwithstanding whatever may be said to the contrary, a mystery overhangs every epizootic disease, giving rise to vague and contradictory actions in reference to its precise cause. Now upon this point, as well as upon the point of the nature and treatment of influenza, it will be observed as we proceed that I have dared to step out of the beaten track of routine and have dared to advance some new theories. I am not abandoning the cause of science and progress by uttering these sentiments. I believe the question to be a question between progress and retrogression, and the issue we have to try is of enormous importance. In the first place it is quite safe to conclude that this distemper, which has ravaged the whole of England and most parts of Europe during the past winter (1864), emanates from atmospheric causes acting directly upon the organic system of the nerves. But what the precise nature of that cause is, our finest tests in science have as yet failed to detect.

The conclusions that I have come to are as follows: firstly, that the state of the system which we are in the habit of designating "influenza" is *not* of itself a disease at all ; it is simply a sequence or particular condition of the constitution in which there is an absence of the requisite quantity of nervous energy, deranging the vital principle and inciting irritability; secondly, that the system does not become affected through the medium of respiration, but through the medium of the skin. I cannot bring my mind to believe that epizootics of this nature are dependent upon some disproportion of oxygen in the air, or to the presence of sulphuretted hydrogen of oxone, nor yet to any organic or inorganic morbific matter in the air. I should rather attribute it to some change or modification in the magnetical or electrical state of the atmosphere, altering its relations to the living body. I will give you my reasons for these conclusions. If the epizootic was propagated through the medium of respiration, the tissues which had come first in contact with the poison or irritant in its unspent or undiluted form would, as a matter of course, suffer the most. If a horse or a man takes an irritant poison, of which he dies, what do we find ? Why, intense inflammation of the mucous membranes of the stomach and bowels. If a horse or man is half-suffocated in the fumes of dense smoke, so that in a few days he dies, what do we find ? Why, intense inflammation of the mucous membranes of the air passages, and congestion of the lungs ; in either case we find that the very tissues which have come into direct actual contact with

the irritant are most severely affected. So should we find
it in influenza if it was caused by some irritant or morbific poison in the air.   But what does *post mortem* examinations of true influenza cases prove to us ?   They
show us unmistakably that fine delicate membranes in the
air cells are nearly always perfectly free from disease. Frequently we find these tissues in a state the very reverse
of congestion, inflammation, or tumefaction.   They are of
a lighter colour, are less in weight, less in bulk, than when
in health, and even in those cases where we have
hydrothorax *hydrops pericardu,* this has not been preceded by the slightest inflammatory action it has
exhaled out of the surfaces and not exuded.   I look
upon these as almost, if not quite, proof positive
that it is not attributable to a morbific poison or to a
prutrescence in the atmosphere. I am of opinion that the
true cause of influenza must be looked for in the peculiar
condition of the atmosphere, and the favourable state of
the skin and coat in the animal itself.   I consider that
the primary cause of this epizotic, is a deficiency of electricity in the atmosphere during the whole of the period
the distemper is prevalent ; and that during the time
that such deficiency exists an insensible influence is ex-
erted upon all animals, and the degree they are affected
is in proportion to their susceptibility and favourable condition.   The effects it produces is in the first place felt in
the nervous system, and secondly in the vascular system.
The manner in which it affects the system is by robbing it
of a certain quantity of animal electricity in order to effect
equilibrium. A chill is experienced while this extracting
process is going on, a creeping sensation is felt in every

part, the horse experiences a pricking sensation frequently attended with rigour, the system being in a perfectly passive state during this time. I consider the abstraction of the invigorating principle is not confined to the solids, but the vital fluids also. There is a loss of animal heat, the skin is cold, and if it is permitted to go on radiating, the whole system soon becomes thoroughly affected, and the vital powers are thrown prostrate, partaking somewhat of a state of torpidity. It must not be forgotten that the skin is a perfect network of nervous filaments, and that these nervous filaments have both direct and indirect connection with all the nervous centres, and through them with every vital organ in the body. My own experience has proved to me that influenza is not dependent upon a low temperature of the air. If cold weather was of itself an exciting cause, we should always find the greatest number of fresh cases on the day or the day after an intensely cold day and night, whereas we do not find that to be the case. I have found nearly as many fresh cases during the prevalence of beautifully fine, dry, warm weather, with a clear crisp atmosphere, as in a wet, dull, murky atmosphere. I mean during the whole time the epizootic is prevalent. A long continuance of east winds may possibly contribute some of the conditions necessary to its development, but of this I am persuaded whenever epizootic disease is prevalent, the mystery is dependent upon some invisible subtle agency operating from without, and exists in the atmosphere. I do not wish to be understood that the whole force of the attack is instantaneous. Supposing an animal in perfect health, and in tip-top condition, surrounded and pressed upon by an atmosphere which is in this peculiar state, the rapidity and intensity of the attack will depend upon the state of the skin and coat of such animal. As to its acting as a good conductor or non-conductor if the animal has a thick coat or is clothed too much, inducing a damp state of the coat, and whilst in this state permitted to stand in a cold stable, or outside in the open air, that is the precise time the mischief is done.

There is no process of incubation in this affection. If all the conditions are favourable to radiation, the system can contract the infection suddenly, and become affected to a degree entitling it to the term of influenza in five minutes; but if the conditions are not so favourable, it will require twenty or thirty minutes' exposure to the same trying circumstances to produce the same effect, and in some less susceptible animals they may tolerate the same influence for several days before becoming affected. I am decidedly of opinion that some horses are not susceptible to its influence, and even those that are, after they have passed through it, with very rare exceptions, enjoy an immunity from it. It would appear that the constitution had become inured or accommodated to it, for they enjoy perfect health after, and this, too, in the same atmosphere. Horses occupying the most healthy and best ventilated stables are equally liable to contract the complaint, but there is this difference, it is less malignant and less fatal. It is a fact that at other times the animals may experience a chill, and have a check of perspiration, and the result will be an ordinary catarrhal affection. But when this subtle agency exists in the air and is exerting itself, another phenomenon is witnessed of an entirely different nature, and of essentially typhoid tendencies, the distinguishing mark or effect of which is an unusual, peculiar, and general weakness, a most susceptible system, and the small, feeble character of the pulse.

Is influenza contagious and infectious? My own experience leads me to the belief that it is not. During the last ten years I have had upwards of one hundred cases of undoubted influenza, and have watched it very closely, yet up to the present time I have never seen one single clear case of the affected animal communicating the distemper. I have had cases of young horses in the farm yard all running together, drinking out of the same trough, eating out of the same manger; some of them have had influenza, and others not. We frequently see one or more horses in a large stable affected, and the horse in the stall next to the worst case perfectly healthy. I must remind my readers that contagion, strictly speaking, implies the capability of certain diseases being produced by actual contact of the healthy animal with some part of the one labouring under disease, and not through the medium of the atmosphere. On the other hand, infection is the word used to denote the propagation of maladies through the medium of the air, which becomes charged with the contaminating principle given off in the form of exhalations from the diseased animal, and which excites the like disease in those animals that are subject to its influence, they being predisposed to take the malady. Now I come to the nature of influenza. Most influenzas have been

D

noted for affecting severely the mucus membranes of the
air passages, but in the epizootic of 1872, the most fatal
year in New York with only rare exceptions, nothing of
the kind occurred.   Their phases varied in several points
of detail, but they had all many points in common.   I
have before me a treatise on influenza in the horse, written
by Mr. Spooner, of Southampton, in the year 1837.   It
contains not only his views, but also an ably written
essay upon the same subject, written by Professor Sewell.
A valuable discussion ensued, in which we have the
opinions of Professor Spooner, Messrs. Field, Turner,
Youatt, Dickins, Braly, Cheetham, Sibbald, and Ainslie.
The treatise also contains the opinion of Stewart William
Percival, Karkeek, and others.   I have taken great pains
and trouble to peruse the whole of these valuable opinions
and many others, written in the *Veterinarian,* and works
of other authors, many of which are to be found in the
library in the South Kensington Museum, to many of
which I am indebted for my knowledge.   I find Professor
Sewell and Karkeek and some other eminent men
attribute "influenza" to a meteoric or volcanic origin.
Many of them view it as inflammatory in its nature ; but
since that period times have changed men's views upon
this and many other diseases, and a change has also taken
place in the type of disease.   We very rarely now see a
clear well-defined case of local inflammation.   In the
present day the constitution of neither man nor animal
can tolerate the old-fashioned treatment.   Enlightened
and scientific men have discovered that in the present day
a milder plan of treatment is more successful, to the
honour of Mr. William Haycock and Mr. E. A. Friend,

they being the first who discerned and had the moral courage to propagate this great truth. Influenza is an Italian word, meaning influence. Its primary action is direct upon the nervous system, and secondly upon the vascular system. The animal appears to be suddenly deprived of the requisite quantity of vigour or vital stimulus necessary for the due performance of the vital actions. I am of opinion that the whole system suffers alike, not only the vital organs, viz., the brain, heart, lungs, liver, &c., but every living tissue in the whole frame is deficient in nerve force or animal electricity. The first observable symptoms are cold skin, loss of appetite, dulness, listlessness, pulse small and feeble, varying from 60 to 80 or even 100 in one minute; breathing not always disturbed, a prickling uneasiness in the legs and feet, an excitable, susceptible state of the bowels, voiding fæces frequently, which are soft and scanty; in some few cases we have spontaneous diarrhœa. These symptoms are followed by swollen eyelids, weeping, in some severe cases effusion of lymph into the chambers of the eye. The mouth is not particularly hot, neither are the membranes highly injected. There is more or less swelling about the legs and fetlocks; this is accompanied by a morbid capillary action generally. It assumes and proceeds in a uniform course, and not by natural and distinct stages. I feel no doubt many of these cases experience headache to a very great extent, from the manner in which they will lay their heads upon your breast and seem to find relief in their heads being stroked. In some cases for months after the attack, symptoms approaching to megrims hang about them, rendering them completely useless; these fits occasionally seizing them if "backed" or their heads raised suddenly, when they stagger and fall. No doubt this results from a thickening of the membranes of the brain, causing an effusion into the ventricles. The late Professor Dick, of Edinburgh, showed me a case in which bleeding, laxatives, alteratives, vegetable and mineral tonics had been tried in vain, but the employment of setons over the front of the head and behind the poll for three weeks completely restored it. The organ which suffers chiefly is the heart. But it is the result of a state of things the very opposite of congestion or inflammation; it is affected mechanically, not from diseased actions. It is deprived of its wonted vigour; it is unable to empty itself in its systolic and disastolic action. A portion of the blood remains in the ventricles, the heart is feebly but irritably labouring, agitating, and beating upon the same charge of blood over and over again. The fibrine of the blood attaches itself to the tricuspid and bicuspid valves and their cords, as well as the corded tendinea and cortina tendinea, by which (the passages being to a certain extent choked at every involuntary contraction of the ventricles) an escape of blood back into the ventricles takes place. This state of the central pump will account for the diminished if not suspended force from behind, and hence the small, feeble, and almost bloodless pulse. This was pointed out to me by the great friend of my boyhood, the late Professor Dick, of Edinburgh, upwards of twenty years ago. There is another symptom, which in some cases occurs in a most remarkable degree; 1 allude to the great irregularity or intermittency of the pulse. Mr Haycock says, "I have observed it in some

cases so great that there has been a total omission of
pulsation for five or six seconds, and this occurrence will
be repeated three or four times every minute. This
peculiarity will exist all through its illness, and often
for three or four months after its recovery." I do not
consider this of very great importance, though it is an
exceedingly interesting coincidence to notice and to contemplate. I always view it as a favourable omen. I
consider it results from nervous debility, and fully believe
that where there is an intermittent pulse there exists
a clot of blood in the heart. How often do we find horses
affected with influenza dying rather unexpectedly ? What
is the explanation of it ? *Post-mortem* examinations
show that there was neither active nor chronic disease in
any vital organs to cause death nor yet rupture. Of the
human being it would be said that he died of spasm
of the valves of the heart. I have no doubt that in every
case life passes away in the tranquil sleep of death
through the medium of sinking and syncope. In some
few cases it would appear that the whole virulence of the
disease concentrates itself in some local superficial part—
the legs or between the lower maxillary bone, where deep,
sloughing ulcers occur, and even in a vital organ, as-
suming a putrescent character, as if death of the parts
had taken place.

These cases generally do badly; there is not a
sufficiency of vitality to see them through. Whenever
the animal begins to lie down it is generally a favourable
sign, as when they are recovering they generally lie
down a good deal. It is also noticed that those who
swell most about the eyes generally get on the most

Sometimes we find symptoms of complicated influenza. By this term we mean horses with some previous disease upon them becoming affected with influenza, or else whilst suffering from an attack of influenza it assumes a malignant, subacute form, locating itself in some vital organ. In either case they are dangerous, and will be found most difficult cases to treat. They are intractable and often running on to tuberculous lungs or effusion. Some of them are not bad to diagnose. There are cases in which the pulse is kept up by debility solely. These can be discriminated and must not be mistaken for complicated cases; there is an unusually foul, clammy mouth, offensive odour, dirty, yellow, buccal membranes and conjunctive. You cannot by any means produce and maintain healthy reaction; the bowels are sluggish, the faeces dry, hard, and coated, the secretions generally suspended, the diseased organ will feel the full force of the deficiency of animal electricity, and the result in most cases is that parenchyma of the organ yields to the putrid stage, and death, in from seven to ten days, closes the scene. We will now examine this question from another point of view, so that my readers may have the fullest investigation into the nature of influenza. We will follow our patient to the knacker's yard and there make a careful *post-mortem* examination, and what do we find? In complicated cases we meet with a great variety of disorganizations and lesions, most extensive and dreadful alterations in the structures, generally in the lungs, effusion of lymph outside the pericardium, and fibrinous attachments of the pleura. In simple influenza it is perfectly immaterial whether the subject is an old horse or a young one, whether it be in a high fleshy condition or in a low and lean condition. If it has died from influenza, there will be no trace whatever of disease in any vital organ obvious to the anatomist; but there will be one leading feature invariably present, viz., a soft, flabby, pulpy condition of all the muscular structures throughout the body and the whole of the vital organs. These tissues are blanched and of a pale clay colour, as if the whole system had been blighted, blasted, and the fire of vitality had burned out, leaving a white ash only, and that the arterial blood had lost its vermilion colour. To render my views more clear, I will illustrate it by two examples. I have spoken of nerve forces : we all know that a palsical limb is consequent upon either complete or partial loss of nerve power. If a *post-mortem* examination be made of a limb recently palsical it is found that the flesh is soft, flabby, pulpy, and of a pale clay colour, exactly the same as we find in cases that have died of influenza. Again, if we examine a body that has been killed by lightning, being in perfect health, there is the same soft, flabby, pulpy state of the flesh, which is of a pale clay colour, exactly the same as found in influenza subjects. To call the particular condition of the muscular structures disease, is, I maintain, a fallacy. I contend, and in this I am supported by many eminent veterinary surgeons, that being struck down by lightning, and being attacked by influenza is precisely the same thing in nature ; the same vital element is ab-

stracted in the one case, as is abstracted in the other.
There is no doubt whatever that in those cases struck by
lightning, they are instantaneously and completely
deprived of animal electricity, and the function of vitality
ceases at once. Influenza is only a modified form of this
very phenomenon; the one is instantaneous and complete, the other gradual, imperceptible, and incomplete,
fortunately affording an opportunity at this important
and critical juncture for the prudent surgeon to step in,
and by the employment of wise and well-considered
treatment, to fan the flickering flame of life until Nature
rallies, reaction is established, and life saved. I now
approach the most important part of my subject, the
treatment of complicated and simple influenza. In all
cases it is advisable to obtain the services of a practical
veterinary surgeon, but the mode of treatment given in
these pages has been frequently and successfully tried by
the author, as well as by many veterinary surgeons.
We will take complicated influenza first. This, in a
practical point of view, is a question that demands a
more careful consideration than any other, as the very
life of our patient depends upon our correct diagnoses.
There are many cases that require all the practice, ability,
and enlightened judgment we can exercise to clearly
comprehend them. How I wish I was endowed with a
stronger intelligence that would enable me to clear away
all the mist that surrounds this part of my subject. I
have devoted much time upon this matter for a number
of years, yet I find the more I study the more I have to
learn. But of this I think it is fully demonstrated, that
influenza is not the fault of the groom, as too many

gentlemen and practitioners are very ready to assert. We will presume that we have decided in our own minds that our patient is one that comes under the denomination of complicated influenza—that is, influenza located in some vital organ and assumed a malignant type. What is the best treatment to be adopted—first, is vivisection or vesication indicated? The impression upon my own mind is that they are not. The conclusion I have formed during a pretty extensive experience, in large studs, and among heavy cart and dray horses, is that nature will not tolerate coercion, and that it can repair damages much better than we can do. It does it in less time and much more effectually by vital force, which has a greater curative power than any other remedy possesses. What Nature does is done spontaneously, if we only give her fair play. I am quite satisfied that bleeding is dangerous, and should not be attempted under any circumstances. My deceased father told me of a great outbreak of influenza when he was in the army, when bleeding was largely resorted to, with a result of the loss of ninety-five per cent. of the patients. This treatment should never be resorted to while we possess such drugs as aconite. Counter-irritation is also to be deprecated if used severely to the throat and sides; yet much benefit is derived from a gentle stimulating with mustard, or, as Mr. Mavor advocates, mustard and linseed meal. By condemning blisters — I mean fly blisters—I must give a reason for doing so. In the first place, we create an additional inflammation, doubling the constitutional disturbance, driving the blood with increased fury through the system, especially through the diseased organs, helping to exhaust and break down their structure, and thereby cause irreparable damage. Another serious evil is that we have sympathetic disturbance from absorption of the fly. I have always adopted mustard in the early stages of influenza, and with marked effect. Mr. Mavor, I am told, uses the vapour bath with great success. In many cases I have derived much benefit from giving the patient sulphate of magnesia in four-ounce doses twice a day, as a febrifuge, alterative, and purifier. Rowels and setons are sometimes used, but do more harm than good. . . . . . . In therapeutics my mode of proceeding is similar to that which I adopt in simple influenza; keep the patient's head to the open door day and night, and give stimulating tonic. Some practical veterinary surgeons give iodide of potassium, and also chlorate of potass, but not having given them myself I cannot speak of their effects. Diuretic medicine is undoubtedly good in removing œdema and other deposits, but have no power to arrest the process of effusion and exudations. Contradictory as it may appear to my readers, I incline to the opinion that if the real truth could be fully known, it would be found that effusion is actually facilitated during the action of diuretic medicine. This is known, that during the action of cathartic medicine, which abstracts the watery part of the blood by way of the bowels, as diuretics do by the kidneys, the earthral action (the process of effusion) goes on more rapidly. Some patients will rally to a certain point, then become stationary for several days, the pulse standing at 60, 72, or 80, the symptoms neither indicating

progression nor retrogression; still neither the accelerated breathing nor pulse settles at all. In a few cases
this is purely referable to weakness, but if the secretions
and mucous membranes are unsatisfactory this is an
ugly symptom. Without for one moment understanding
the importance of attending to this point, it is of the
utmost consequence to act judiciously, for an error made
now throws all chances against the patient. Two drachms
of aloes, or eight of oil, given at this stage, especially if
the bowels are comparatively empty, is sufficient to kill
the largest and best horse alive. The aloes get absorbed
into the system and act as a deadly poison, or else their
action is followed by constipation.

Always rely upon enemas, frequent draughts of cold
water, and, if it is eating moderately, one drachm of
aloes, or half a drachm of calomel, or, which I like far
better, two ounces of linseed oil. Under such circumstances you can make no progress until the bowels
are corrected. Sometimes the pulse will rise daily in
the face of camphor and belladonna, but upon dis-
continuing them and giving tonic stimulants, the pulse
at once commenced to excel, and my patient recovered,
but after all most of them die. I now approach influenza simple. This is the most important part to
my readers of this subject. If the horse is observed
just as it is in the act of contracting the epizootic, and
when it is in its incipient stage, if proper care is at
once supplied, it will be found that it is only an
ephemeral disturbance. In such a case administer a
pint of warm ale, one table-spoonful of ground ginger
(Barbadoes is best), and the same quantity of powdered

aniseed. The effect produced is so satisfactory, in nearly every case, that it would appear to be the very stimulant required at the time. Any diffusible stimulant that acts on excitement, such as brisk exercise or considerable friction to the skin, is of great benefit. Get the skin thoroughly warm, supply it with cool fresh air, and you have a reaction established immediately. The progress of affection is arrested. The system seems to assume altered electrical conditions, but it is not to be supposed that this neutralises the invisible influence which is exerting itself from without, but it excites and maintains an artificial spirit of vitality, which enables the system to withstand the shock it has sustained in the loss of electricity, which, unlike the process of equilibrium, is being completed. If some hours have elapsed and the vesculate system has become involved, administer spirit nitrous ether, and tincture pimento, one ounce of each in four ounces of warm water every six hours. Sometimes great benefit is derived by changing medicine, if so the following can be given instead—spirit nitrous ether one ounce, sig· ammonia acetatus one ounce. Keep the horse's head tied to the open door. The legs and feet are generally hot and tender, and will keep themselves warm, and the simple pressure of a bandage causes pain. Regulate the quantity of clothing to the heat of the skin, as you may do much mischief by smothering the skin with too much clothing, by increasing the fever and causing your patient to commence blowing· There are some cases in which the patient cannot tolerate diaphoreosis. Unless the horse has pumiced feet remove the shoes, if the pain in the legs is considerable, put them in warm water, use arnica lotion, one part in ten of water. In the worst cases great relief is given by putting on a patten shoe and thus raising the heel of the foot. There are some cases that do better with carbonate of ammonia, and pulverised ginger, one drachm each every six hours. It is necessary to watch its effects, and it must be discontinued after a certain point is gained. After a few doses the salivary glands become acted upon, and no doubt the glandular system throughout the body is more or less stimulated by it. It is a beautiful stimulant to the nerves of the stomach and chest, it does not nauseate, but will produce a nice pultaceous state of the bowels, and cleanses all the membranes. If continued too long or given in too large doses it will produce purging. I believe we can accomplish everything with it that we can with calomel, except nausea and salivation. Where fever runs very high, pulse 80 or 92, give extract of belladonna one drachm twice a day. If the patient is under my own care, I prefer giving ten-drop doses in one table-spoonful of water every hour, but this cannot always be done with all patients; then large doses morning and night are given. If the patient has sore throat, the medicine should not be given in a drink form. In cases where the animal has a thick coat, clipping will have a magical effect. As to diet, one quart of cold water every hour, linseed tea, malt mashes, swede turnip, carrot, oat straw with the oats in it, plenty of wild mint, if it can be got, fresh grass, or a little sweet hay. Give anything so that you can keep the animal feeding. It will be gathered from what I advance that it is to the secret processes of

nature, and not so much to the action of medicine, that
the credit of the most successful cases belongs ; and, as I
view the beautiful theory of health and disease, this conclusion is forced upon me, that man in his shortsight-
edness, his vanity, and selfishness, has never sufficiently
comprehended and appreciated the great fundamental
truth, that nature is ever a wise economist, doing all
things well.   Having wandered from my subject in treating " Influenza " at great length, I will now turn to the
feeding of the horse.   In feeding, the motto should be—
quality not quanity, as in every bushel of oats, the
heavier the weight the less husk there is to the bushel.
In feeding the cart or farm horse it is a good
plan to cut all its food into chaff.   The quantity
each horse ought to have is just as much as it can eat,
without leaving any in its manger, this is a good system
to go by, let the horse measure its own stomach.   In
Scotland the cart horses are fed in the following mann er
and I have never seen a better plan ; they take, say two
trusses of hay, two of clover, ten sheaves of oats un-
thrashed, and cut them all up together, mixing a little
common salt with it, about 1 lb., to the above quantity,
when the horses are fed a little bean and pea meal is
mixed with the cut food, and if slightly damped, about
four pounds of meal per day with the above mixture of
cut food will keep the heavy cart horse in good condition.
The Kentish farmers are, as a rule, good horse keepers ;
they uuderstand that two horses well fed will do more
work than three half starved. The Hertfordshire farmers,
on the other hand, would lead one to believe from the
horses we see in the waggons and at plough, that they

undertake to build horses as many contractors do houses ; run up the frames and bare walls, and then sell them to other people to put the plaster on ; or perhaps they are of a philosophic turn of mind, and would answer as Butterwick did, when twitted about his horse, " Who wants to see a horse even from stem to stern ? No, sir ; it is monotonous and wearisome to the mind. Which is best, a level plain, or landscape with a little bit of hill and a little bit of valley ? You have it in a horse like mine ; and, beside, you are always sure that nobody has stolen a single, solitary bone, and you have all you pur-chased. If he was as fat as a bladder of lard, how should we know that some of its most important bones were not missing?" The carriage horse and hunter should always be fed on the best old oats, with white peas or beans, or what is better, both. Some people will say that old beans make horses legs fill; depend upon it, they oftener fill for the want of them. Four quarterns of oats and one of beans, is as much as one horse will eat in a day as a rule, if he is in good condition, with a little sweet hay morning and night. I always give cut hay with the corn, as it makes the horse masticate his food better ; he does not swallow the corn whole, as some greedy feeders are apt to do. I do not think clover good for horses in fast work, but am fond of good sanfoin to cut up. Mouldy and mow-burnt hay are very injurious to the horse ; the first will be sure to make the animal thick-winded and ultimately go broken-winded. It produces irritation in the air cells by the fungal growth of mould, and mow-burnt hay is equally bad, as it acts powerfully upon the kidneys, often causing that terrible complaint diabetes. It is therefore necessary that every groom should be careful about the quality of food sent for the horses under his care. No groom, however skilful he may be, can train horses upon bad hay and fusty oats. It is a great mistake to buy oats for hunters and carriage horses, and certainly for cab-horses, that weigh less than 42 lbs. per bushel, for every pound you gain in weight it is in meal ; the heavier the oat the thinner the husk. Sometimes horses are off their feed from debility after some illness, and require the stomach toning down and the nerves bracing ; for such it is necessary to give a powerful tonic to help nature to reassert itself. For the benefit of my readers who may have horses suffering from nervous debility, I have placed in the hands of Messrs. Perks and Lewellwn, chemists, Hitchin, a valuable recipe, with *carte blanche* to supply them to their customers with full instructions, having every confidence that they will restore the diges-tive organs and make them fulfil their proper functions.

The hunter being the most valuable to the tenant farmer and small breeder—as a good sound and clever hunter is always as good as ready money— therefore it will not be out of place to give a few hints of how to breed them, and also how to train them to make perfect horses in the field. In selecting the mare to breed from, it is necessary to make as much enquiries into her lineage as it is possible to obtain. First examine her carefully to ascertain if she has any hereditary complaints, and if the mare has curby hocks, splints, thick wind, a roarer, or imperfect vision, discard her at once however good she may be, for her progeny is sure to inherit its mother's failings. If, on the other hand, the mare has flat legs, good feet (if rather large it is a good fault), if the sole is not flat, deep chested, a good oblique shoulder, rather long in the back, with powerful loins, the fore limbs standing well forward, and of six or seven years of age (not under six or over twelve), you may come to the conclusion that you have a chance for a good foal. But look back to her ancestors and try and find out if any of them were screws, for the best mares will sometimes throw back for five or six generations. It is a noticeable fact that the best horses of the present age were the progeny of sires and dams of moderate pretension; for instance, Queen Mary, the mother of Blink Bonny, was only called a fourth-class mare, and before breeding Blink Bonny was sold for £20. Then, again, we find the dam of Robert the Devil only a miserable plater, yet both these mares were of sound pedigree, no screws being found among their ancestors. The mare having been decided on as a fit subject for the honour of brood mare, we must look for the horse best adapted for getting hunters. When speaking of unsound mares, I mean mares with hereditary failings. A mare may only have three legs, and yet be fit for breeding purposes; if her lameness is the result of an accident and not of hereditary causes, the mare may be considered sound. The horse should be sixteen hands in height, of a good colour, with lofty fore-hand, a neck as light as possible (yet short-necked horses are generally clear-winded), clear wide jaws and nostrils, large and thin shoulders, strong and muscular thighs, deep chest, and short backs;

above all his joints should be strong, firm, and closely
knit. His legs and pasterns should be rather short, and
the cannon flat, the feet rather large and sound. Horses
with round legs never wear, and are sure to go lame; long
hind-legged horses can never gallop down hill or take
bold leaps with weight on their backs without flounder-
ing and coming to grief. Having found both mare and
horse good, we may naturally expect a good foal, and to
make a good foal a clever hunter, we must commence
with it at his mother's side, by handling as previously
described. We have to bring out its jumping powers,
as it is this point on which much of its value depends,
so we must teach it to jump naturally. For this purpose
we feed the mare in a yard, and at the gateway lay down
a row of faggots, hazel, or soft wood; never put thorns so
that the mare and foal have to jump over them every
time they go to feed. This should be continued as long
as the foal is at its mother's side. After it is taken away
from the mare, the jump can be gradually heightened
and widened, until it has a square yard to clear, then it
must be doubled by placing another row of faggots in
front of the first, making the two about eight feet apart,
letting the foal have to jump in and out like a cat. Next
use it to go down a made road with a ditch cut across,
and a bank made of the earth cut from the ditch. If
these tactics are followed up you will have a natural
jumper before the saddle is put on his back; but upon
no account let boys have anything to do with it, as
they will drive the foal to see it jump, and there is more
harm done in fun than hard work. When the young
horse is put to fences, after it is properly broken to the

saddle, it should be led over with a man on its back for the first time or two, until it thoroughly understands what is wanted of it by its rider. Never put a funky man on a young horse: he is sure to spoil it and make it refuse its fences; it is oftener the fault of the man than the horse that it does not jump. You may often hear in the field gentlemen say, "I can't get this brute to jump;" they are generally those that can gallop through a line of gates or down a lane, but cannot get their hearts high enough to take a sheep hurdle. They are like a well-known old sportsman, near Melton Mowbray, who used to hunt up to his eightieth year, and when he came to a flight of rails, would say to his groom, "Tom, knock the top rail off." When that was done, he would say, "Knock another off, and I'll go over if I break my neck." These gentlemen somehow or other seem to always get good horses, and when they have them they have not pluck to ride them. Hunters, from the nature of their work, are liable to meet with many injuries from which other horses are exempt, among which are thorns, overreach, blows from rails, and striking one leg against the other when galloping through heavy ground. This is often the cause of splint, one of the most troublesome kinds of lameness, for the horse is often lame with splint, and being in its incipient form, it does not set up enough local inflammation to enable the unskilful to find out its seat, and many horses are said to be lame in the shoulder when it is an incipient splint below the knee that causes the mischief. Some cases have come under my observation, in which, although the animal has not been able to put its foot to the ground, the cause has been a splint not larger than a grain of wheat close up under the knee, and could be detected only by an excited action of the pulse over the part affected. This sort of thing often causes the groom and owner much anxiety; knowing the horse to be lame and being unable to find the cause, it is put down to everything but the right. It will be called chest founder, chronic founder, shoulder pitched, and many other things. When a boy I once asked the late Professor Dick what was chronic founder, and was told it was a very convenient phrase to use when you have a horse lame in the foot and cannot find the seat of lameness. "We call it," said the Professor, "chronic founder, and send many fools away satisfied." The symptoms of splint lameness are pointing the foot, resting the toe only upon the ground ; the horse has great difficulty in moving forward, cannot bend its knee, but can go back, which a horse lame in the shoulder cannot do. The cause of splint is the formation of a tumour under the *periasteum*, or membrane which covers the bone. During the growth of the tumour this becomes stretched to an unnatural degree, and causes the animal great pain, owing to the sensitive nature of this covering. It is difficult to conceive how splint should appear on the outside of the small bones, except, we suppose, the space between these bones is occupied by mechanism of an important character. It is much easier to account for their almost exclusive appearance on the inside of the limb, the inner splint bone being situated nearer the central part of the body than the other, and from the nature of its connection with the knee it is subject to a greater proportion of weight than the outer one, hence it is more liable to injuries and inflammation, consequently inducing this bony deposit which has been termed splint. The inner bone supports the entire weight which is transmitted to one of the small knee bones ; it is the only support of that bone, while but a portion of the weight is sustained by the outer splint bone, and the pressure is divided between it and the cannon bone. Many smiths, who are but imperfectly acquainted with their profession, most absurdly elevate the outer heel of the shoe, which throws an additional weight on the inner splint bone. Splints very often are the result of a blow given with the inside of the foot, and when a splint is suspected, that part of the leg should be rubbed for three or four days with strong mercurial ointment ; this will soften the tumour and make it porous; then it should be blistered with Mr. Gregory's famed vesico sudorific, which will speedily remove the splint by absorption. . . . . Overreaches are the result of the horse placing the toe of the hind foot upon the heel of the fore foot, long hind-legged horses are very guilty of doing this when jumping into heavy land; they cannot get their fore feet out of the way soon enough, and the toe of the hind foot, striking the heel with great force, sometimes will cut the heel nearly off. If the wound is large, it is often troublesome. The first thing to do with an overreach is to wash clean with warm water, examine carefully and make sure there is no foreign substance in the wound. If the piece cut down with the foot is nearly off, and is only of a horny substance, do not hesitate to cut it off, for it will heal much sooner with it off than if kept on. If, however, the wound is deep, after it has been carefully washed, and you **are** satisfied there is no dirt or other substance in the wound, get some carbolic oil made with one part pure carbolic acid, and five parts finest Lucca or salad oil, pour some into the wound, then press the lips of the wound as close together as possible, and if you can put a stitch into it with a curved needle to hold the lips together, it will greatly facilitate the healing process.

Having got the lips together, saturate a pellet of tow with the oil, bandage it firmly over the wound, and do not remove the bandage again for three or four days, by which time the wound will have become consolidated. Sometimes the leg will swell very much, and masters and grooms fear that the leg is too tightly bandaged and undo it too soon, causing the wound to slough, and leave an ugly scar for their pains. When legs swell from the inflammation set up by the wound, it can easily be prevented from rising up the leg to the body by puncturing the swollen mass with the lancet in three or four places; this will let out the inflammatory fluid and arrest the swelling. The limb should be bathed with arnica lotion composed of arnica b.p. one part, and cold spring water ten parts. Keep the limb moist with linen bandages soaked with the lotion ; never let them get dry, or you will do much more harm than good. It is better to have the legs washed with the lotion and no bandages put on than to let the bandage get dry. Short-legged horses very seldom overreach, but long-legged ones often do—to their owner's cost, and risk of neck and collar-bone, &c.

THORN.

This is another troublesome customer to the groom, for often it is in the horse's legs some days before it can be detected. But every groom after a day's hunting should examine very carefully the legs to ascertain if there are thorns in them; the two worst and most likely places for a thorn to be is in the knee joint and the coronet between the hair and hoof. Sometimes a horse will get punctured with a thorn so deep in the joint that it will cause synovia or joint oil to run, and when this occurs, under the best treatment, there is sure to be an enlargement of the joint. Often a limb is pierced with a thorn and the point broken off and left in the wound. This is more troublesome than a large thorn left in, for the latter is soon detected, and when once pulled out causes but little trouble; while a very small piece of thorn, especially black thorn, from its acid nature, will set up inflammation and suppuration, sometimes to a great extent before the evil is found out, as many grooms are apt to mistake a swelling from a thorn for a rap with a rail in the hunting-field. If there is any doubt about a swelling being caused by a blow or a thorn, the leg should be examined minutely. The best way to do this is to take a knife and draw the blade slowly up against the hair and examine the skin as you proceed. If you find a puncture only as large as the eye of a needle, probe the wound to see if any thorn is there; if you cannot find one, rub into the hole a small quantity of Gregory's vesico sudorific; this will keep the wound open and set up a discharge, and if a thorn is there it will draw it out; if there is no thorn it will act

as a counter-irritant and prevent suppuration. Sometimes a thorn can be seen, yet it is so deep that it
cannot be taken hold of even with a pair of forceps ; to
take a thorn out under these circumstances, you must
put a small key over the thorn and press tightly so as to
force the thorn up the pipe of the key and enable you to
lay hold of it with the forceps.   Another thing of the
thorn class, only worse, is a stub.   This is met with by
the horse putting its foot upon newly-cut brushwood, in
going through gaps in hedgerows, or through newly-cut
woods.   Sometimes they inflict wounds that are very
deep, often going through the sole of the foot and
lamella to the coffin bone.   Many valuable horses have
died of tetanus or lockjaw, from the effect of a wound
of this class.   As soon as the groom finds a stub in the
horse's foot he should have its shoe taken off, and the
hoof round the wound cut away with a small sharp knife;
lay the wound well open, probe the wound carefully, and
ascertain if any chip is left behind ; if you find any,
remove it with the forceps, and be quite sure you leave
nothing in the wound.   In probing a wound of this
class, do not use a metal probe, but a gutta-percha one,
as you would be liable to further injure the sensitive
lamella.   Having made sure the wound is clear and
clean, pour into it carbolised oil, put a piece of cotton
wool, saturated with the oil, on the top of the wound,
and bind up.   Remove the wool every morning, and
bathe the wound with warm water, re-dress it and bind
up, and in most cases the animal is well in a few days.
Many persons use tincture of myrrh for wounds, but it
should not be used in deep wounds, as it dries up the

lips and sets up suppuration. The antiseptic treatment of carbolised oil is much better, as its healing qualities are truly wonderful. If a horse has a wound of this class it should have a six-dram purging ball given, its corn stopped, and fed upon carrots, mash, swede, mangold, and sweet hay. Corn would only set up inflammation and be the forerunner of tetanus. Wounds treated with carbolised oil often heal up fast, making too rapid a growth of flesh, and it may be necessary to touch the proud growth with lunar caustic. I never consider that a fault, for after the wound is filled up with new flesh, a touch with the caustic point causes the wound to granulate, forming a skin, and consolidating the injured part.

THE CARRIAGE OR COACH HORSE

Owes its origin to the Cleveland bays, great attention being paid to breeding them in Yorkshire, Durham, and Northumberland, many fine horses of this class being also bred in Lincolnshire. The most useful are those which are propagated by a cross of the Cleveland mare and a thorough-bred horse. These have fine knee actions, lift their feet high, which gives grandeur to their figure and paces; the head is generally well carried, with a beautifully elevated crest, and when they are driven without the bearing rein, they look a really noble horse. Yet such is the force of folly and fashion that the bearing rein—that foul implement of torture—is still upon many a noble steed, and gentlemen will actually tell us that it makes the horse look better. It is a relic of a barbarous age, and the sooner it is placed in the

museum as a relic of the past the less broken knees
and enlargements of the maxilliary glands will be seen
among our horses. It is impossible for the horse with
its head tied to its back to recover itself if it makes
a false step; yet such is the folly and ignorance displayed that we are often told that the bearing rein is
put on to hold the horse up and keep it from stumbling,
To those persons who believe in the use of the bearing
rein, I would advise that they should run over rough
ground with their hands tied behind their backs, and
judge for themseves if they would be able to save themselves if they made a false step. The head acts the same
purpose to the horse as the hands to a man ; if it stumbles
it puts its head out to gain its equilibrium, but if its head
and tail are tied together with the bearing rein and the
animal stumbles he must fall, if the bearing-rein or the
turret does not break.   I have seen many horses drawing
heavy loads up-hill with their heads tied as if in a vice,
making the labour doubly as hard for the poor animals.
Any horse with full liberty will draw a ton better than
it could half-a-ton with its head tied up with the bearing
rein.   Look at a team of horses at plough, drawing up
the face of a steep hill, see how they bend to their work;
they have liberty, consequently they work with ease ;
but see another team with their heads tied up with the
bearing rein, see how hard they labour to draw the
plough, see how often they try to stop, see how they toss
their heads to relieve the strain on the muscles of the
neck; hark how the driver uses the whip to urge them
on, yet fashion has ordained that the horse must suffer
from man's ignorance.   We have a Society for the

Prevention of Cruelty to Animals, and many men are sent to prison for trifling acts of cruelty, yet this great glaring act goes unpunished because it is one of fashion's follies ; and men of education, calling themselves gentlemen, have such a perverted taste that they think it improves the handiwork of the Great Creator. God gave the horse to be the friend and servant of man, but it must have been Satan himself, in his animosity, who played upon the pride and vanity of man, and caused him to invent that piece of abominable torture, the bearing-rein. I hope the day is not far distant when the use of the bearing-rein will become a recognised misdemeanour, and be punished as an act of cruelty. The man bringing such an Act into Parliament would deserve well of his country. An old writer says, " *Dulce et decorum est pro patria mori* ; " yet it is more sweet and honourable to live and do good to our fellow-man by enlightening his mind and exposing the pitfalls and stumbling-stones at his feet. When men are taught the uselessness and cruelty of the bearing rein it will be discarded and become a thing of the past. As the carriage horse is often the sufferer by man's ignorance and by bad shoeing, neglect, and the use of the bearing rein, he often falls, and his knees are badly cut by coming in contact with the hard road. It will be right here to give the reader instructions how to proceed with the horse when its knees are badly broken.

As in all cases of wounds, the first thing is to wash clean with lukewarm water, get all foreign substances out of the wound, then examine carefully by putting the forefinger into the wound to ascertain if the joint is injured; if it is not, dress it with carbolised oil, put on a pellet of tow or cotton wool, and bandage up. If the wound is not very deep, it should not be undone for three days; then the bandage may be taken off, and the wound kept clean, and if dressed with carbolised oil every day, it will soon be well. Horses with broken knees should not have walking exercise until the wounds are nearly well, for fear of opening the wound. If the wound is deep, as is often the case, and a clear fluid running from it resembling glycerine, you can safely conclude that the joint is injured, and that the synovia or joint oil is running. This is very difficult to stop, and in many cases leaves the animal with a stiff joint. The plan I have always adopted when joint oil is running is to fill the wound with lumps of socotorine aloes, put a pellet of tow over the wound dipped in carbolised oil, and bind up. I often fold two *Field* newspapers together and bind them on the horse's leg, they making admirable splints, having substance enough to prevent the horse bending its leg, and easily adapting itself to the shape of the leg without cutting or otherwise injuring the skin. (In cases of accident, if a man breaks his arm or leg, if those near will bind the limb up with a bandage, and use a newspaper or two for splints before attempting to move, many simple fractures will be prevented from becoming compound.) Sometimes the above treatment will not stop the flow of synovia. After being repeated daily for four or five days, it will then be necessary to use strong means—the most effectual is pure carbolic acid. This should be injected into the wound with a small glass syringe, and the wound will heal up unsightly, often leaving a big knee, and many times a stiff joint. After the wound has healed, the knee should be blistered with biniodide of mercury to reduce the gangrenous lump which is sure to form. All horses that have cut their knees deep enough to allow the synovia to escape are never to be trusted again, as they are sure to fall sooner or later. I now come to a very common and also a very trobblesome complaint, known as

LAMINITES,

or fever in the feet. That my readers may thoroughly understand this complaint, it will be necessary that I should give a description of the foot of the horse to show the beautiful handiwork of the Creator, and the ignorance of man, who often look upon the foot of the horse as a solid block of horn, and treats it accordingly. The formation of the foot of the horse fits him above all other animals, except the ass, for the service of man. In short, had the foot of the horse been cleft, it would have been incapacitated from many of the useful departments of its employment, and a correct knowledge of the structures of every part of the foot is indispensably necessary to render us scientific overseers of the farrier's art. The foot externally is composed of the crust, the sole, the bars, and the frog. The crust is that portion which reaches from the termination of the hair to the ground, its greatest depth and thickness is in front, and denominated the toe. It is more shallow at the sides, termed the quarters, and still less behind, termed the heel. In a healthy well-formed foot when the sole is placed upon the ground the front exhibits an angle of forty-five, differing, however, in many horses to the extent of the angle ; still in a healthy foot it is about the fourth part of a semicircle. When the crust has a greater degree of obliquity it is said that the crust has " fallen in," and when the sole is too flat, it is said to be pumiced or convex. If the front be more upright than the above angle it is a sure sign of a contracted foot with the sole too concave. When the crust is deep at the heel it is a foot liable to contraction, thrush, sandcrack, and inflammation. The pastern will be found too upright, and the horse have a very unpleasant action. If, on the other hand, the crust diminished too rapidly from front to back and the heels are low, this is always accompanied by too great obliquity of the pastern, producing a weakness in the joint and liability to sprain the back sinew. The foot itself will be weak and have a tendency to that hidden complaint called navicular joint disease. The general thickness of the crust in front is about half-an-inch, becoming thinner at the quarters and heels. This will show the necessity for shoeing-smiths being adepts at driving nails, seeing the small space they have to nail to. The crust is thinner and a little higher up on the inside than on the outside quarters. This is another wise provision of Nature, because being placed under the inner splint bone more of its weight rests upon the inside than the outside, consequently it is enabled to expand more, and thus, by its elasticity, assists in lessening the force of concussion. The

crust is not liable to much variation in thickness, until
near the top, at the coronet, or where the horn of the
hoof unites with the skin of the pasterns; here it
becomes abruptly thin, and appears as if scooped out;
its colour and consistency also are changed, and it
appears like a continuance of the skin; this thin portion
is called the coronary ring, which covers a thickened
prolongations of the skin called the coronary ligament.
This extension of the skin is supplied with numerous
densely-set blood-vessels, connected together by a fibrous
texture, many of which have the property of secreting
the horny substance which forms the crust. The crust
is composed of numerous fibres which proceed direct
from the coronary to the ground, but which follow an
oblique course from the heel forward; the fibres are
held together by a glutinous substance, which, as before
mentioned, is secreted in the numerous blood-vessels.
The internal parts of the foot are composed of the
laminæ, the sensitive frog, the navicular bone, and the
coffin bone. The laminæ consist of numerous small
horny plates, which line the crust, resembling the
beautiful gills or underpart of a mushroom; these
are arranged with the nicest order and mathematical
precision upon the internal surface of the wall; they
extend in uniform parallels, in a perpendicular direction,
from the top of the hoof at the coronary to the line of
junction of the wall with the sole, and are so thickly set
that no part of the superfices remains unoccupied by
them. They are also continued upon the surface of the
bars, and are soft, yielding, and elastic; but from exposure
become dry and rigid. Every plate exhibits two edges

and two surfaces ; by one edge it grows to the wall, and the other, which is somewhat thinned, hangs loose and floating within the cavity of the hoof. These are two smooth lateral surfaces, and considering the magnitude of the lamilla itself, of enormous extent, so much so that it may be said almost to be constituted of superfices. If we look carefully at the beautiful lamilla lining the foot we must naturally be led to contemplate the great and magnificent designs which Nature evidently had in their formation and very beautiful adaptation, viz., the production of ample surface within a small space, an end that has been obtained by the means of multiplication. The late well-known Thomas Evans, LL.D., made a mathematical calculation of what the united superfices of these lamilla amounted to, and it was found that they afforded an increase of actual surface more than the single internal area of the hoof would give by about twelve times, or about two hundred and twelve square inches, being nearly one square foot and a-half. It is inflammation among this network of delicate mushroom-like fibres that we call laminitis, the destruction of which by disease allows the coffin-bone to drop upon the sensitive sole, the sole in its turn giving way and becoming what is termed drop sole or pumiced feet. The bars are processes of the wall, inflected from its heels obliquely across the bottom of the foot; they extend from the base of the heel into the centre of the foot, between the sole and the frog. They are continuous with the wall or crust with which they form acute angles; anteriorly they stretch as far as the point of the frog, constituting two inner walls between that body and the sole. They seem formed for the purpose of offering resistance to the contractions of the heels. By the side of the bars are two concave surfaces, running from the heel towards the toe; these are called " the cleft of the frog," the surface of which exhibits a remarkable cavity, broad and deep, and of a triangular form. The frog in its superior surface is continuous, uniform, and porous, being the counterpart in form of the inferior surface, presenting only reverses where the one is hollow and the other swelling. Opposite to the cleft is the frog stay, which is elevated and bounded on its sides by two deep channels and a hollow of shallower dimensions in the front. This bold horny elevation is admirably calculated to form that dovetailed connection with the sensitive foot which greatly augments their surfaces of opposition and establishes their union beyond all risk or possibility of dislocation.

The external surface of the sole, or the arched plate forming the bottom of the hoof, and covering the whole of the inferior surface of the foot, excepting the frog, is the part that calls for the undivided attention of the groom. No individual part requires such attention as the sole. As to shoeing, it is here that the smith makes the great mistake of his life, and grooms and owners of horses should see that he does not use the knife to this part; paring the sole of the foot is a vicious practice, and should upon no account be allowed. Many grooms will allow the smith to pare the sole " to clean it out," as they say, not thinking that by that very act they are doing their best to cause the horse to become affected

F

with laminitis. The sole of the horse's foot is only about the sixth of an inch thick after the foot has been deprived of what the shoeing-smith calls the dead horn, but what Nature placed there as a hard wearing substance. That Nature intended it to protect the sole is beyond a doubt, it being devoid of that elasticity which the true sole has, making those flakes the more valuable to the horse as a protection against the stones he has to travel over; yet shoeing-smiths, owners of horses, and grooms, for the sake of making the horse's foot look neat and clean, will have that taken away which God in His wisdom placed there for the mutual benefit of man and horse. Viewed from below, the sole commonly presents an arch of more or less concavity. It is subject to vast variety in degree of the arc: in some feet it is of surprising depth, and in others the arch is converted into a flattened surface, yet both seem to perform equally well. In the hind feet the sole is generally more arched than in the fore, and approaches in figure more of an oval than a circle. That portion elevated from the ground, which forms union with the bars, is nearly double the thickness of the central or circumferent parts, and next to this in substance comes the heel. This is situate at the back part of the foot, at which point the crust of the hoof, instead of being continued round and forming a complete circle, is abruptly bent in. The next in importance to the lamilla of the horse's foot are the cartilages. The cartilages are two broad scabrous concavo-convex cartilaginous plates which surmount the sides and wings of the coffin-bone. There is a groove extending along the upper part of the coffin-bone on each side, except at the protuberance which receives the extensor tendon, and which extends to the very posterior portion of the foot, rising at the quarters fully half-an-inch above the hoof, and diminishing in height backward and forward. These cartilages occupy a greater portion of the foot than the coffin-bone, which they extend far behind, and are fixed into two grooves excavated into the superior lateral borders of the coffin-bone, the navicular bone, and the flexor tendon, and are thus perfectly secured. Below these are other cartilages connected with the under edges of the former, and on both sides of the frog. Between these cartilages is the sensitive frog, occupying the whole of the space, and answering several important purposes, it being an elastic bed upon which the navicular bone and the tendon can play with security, and without concussion to the cartilages. By this means all concussion to the cartilages of the foot are prevented, the cartilages kept asunder, and the expansion of the upper part of the foot preserved. This mechanism is both beautiful and important. The yielding and elastic substance of the frog is pressed upon by the navicular bone, as well as by the tendon and the pattern, and being incapable of condensing itself into less compass is forced out on each side of them and expands the lateral cartilages. These again by their inherent elasticity revert to their former situation when they are no longer pressed outward by the frog. It thus appears that by a different mechanism, but both equally admirable and referable to the same principle of elasticity, the expansion of the upper and lower parts of the hoof are affected ; the one by the descent of the sole and the other by the compression and rising of the frog. The preservation and usefulness of the limbs of the horse are chiefly maintained by this upward expansion. Brown, in his writings, says that "by long-continued pressure on the frog in draught horses, and conveyed from the frog to the cartilage, inflammation is set up and the cartilages turned into bone, viz., sidebone." In this I differ with him, and am of opinion that the more the horse treads upon the frog the better the foot becomes by the attrition. I do not believe that any horse ever had sidebone by treading upon the frog. I believe that he may have them by his heels being elevated by a thick shoe, and all the natural pressure taken off the frog and thrown upon the bars and crust, and by the frog being cut away to make its feet look nice, as if Nature was not in itself perfection. From inferior and posterior sides of the true cartilages, two fibro-cartilaginous processes extend in a forward direction towards the heels of the coffin-bone. They spread inwards upon the surface of the *tendo-perforans,* become united at their inner sides with the superior margin of the sensitive frog, are covered inferiorly by the sensitive sole, and at the same time assist in the support of the sensitive frog. They are triangular in form and are arched in the same manner as the sole. Their use appears to be to fill up the triangular vacant spaces left between the *tendo-perforans* and the heels of the coffin-bone, thereby completing the surface of support for the frog, and extending that for the expansion of the sole. The navicular bone is a small bone resembling a weaver's shuttle and has a side-to-

side movement after the manner of such implement;
hence it is sometimes called the shuttle-bone. One of
the chief uses of this bone appears to be to take off a
portion of the weight from the coffin-bone, and from the
navicular bone it is thrown on the tendon which rests on
the frog beneath. It is on the inner surface of this bone
that the navicular disease first originates ; inflammation
is set up by severe concussion, and being deep-seated,
quite out of the reach of medical and surgical treatment,
the inflammation becomes chronic, the membrane
covering the joint is affected, small tumours form on the
navicular bone, much after the nature of splint; the
navicular bone becomes porous, resembling a piece
of pumice stone, and the animal is lame for life.
Much of this disease is caused by bad shoeing; cutting
and carving the frog and sole have done more to
ruin the horse than all the grooms in Christendom.
Having given a brief outline of the structure
of the foot of the horse, I now propose to show
the principal diseases affecting that important part,
the foot being the foundation, as it is useless to have
a fine top without a foundation. No man would
think of building a mansion without foundations, yet
many gentlemen will buy a fine-top horse without a foot
to stand on, and expect it to carry him through hard
runs, and is dreadfully disappointed if he comes to grief.
No child dreads the fire worse than a groom with a large
stud dreads bad feet ; they are to him a perpetual source
of annoyance. It is his *bête noir* by day and by night,
and his constant prayer is " May my employer always buy
feet, and never buy a horse from a friend." Such is the

honour among some gentlemen (spare the mark !) that if
they have a screw which a respectable dealer will not
buy, they sell it to their friend. The horse soon goes
lame, and then the poor groom has to bear the blame ;
this is often the case with a horse suffering from
laminitis ; he is patched up, his shoes taken off, put on
wet clay, cooling medicine given, coronet blistered, and
after three months' run he is sold to some friend. Look
well to the foot of the horse ; if he has had laminitis the
hoof will be wrinkled like a cow's horn. Many people
when about to sell a horse that has had laminitis or its
companion symtomatic fever will get the smith to rasp
out the rings ; if the foot has been rasped up to the hair,
look upon it with suspicion, for laminitis is a disease so
dreadful in its manifestations, and attended with such
agony and excessive distress to the poor patient, that it
cannot fail to excite compassion for it from all who
witness a case of this terrible type. I can assure my
readers that I myself have been so affected that I would
not—nay, I could not—leave my patient until I was
satisfied that all had been done so far as knowledge lay
within my reach to relieve it at least of some portion of
its sufferings. . . . The first and most obvious
requisite for a practical groom is to possess the faculty to
diagnose a disease when he sees it, to distinguish it from
others manifesting similar symptoms, and forsee its
probable phases and results ; and the author, knowing the difficulties he has had to contend with in his
search after knowledge concerning the horse, wishes to
place his experience in the hands of younger men, to
help them to surmount the difficulties and avoid the

stumbling-stones it has been his lot to fall over. No man, whatever may be his pursuits, deserves the name of a practical man whose knowledge and resources are limited by the experience of his predecessors in a similar walk of life, or who cannot and dare not experiment or reason for himself.

Whatever theories I may advance from time to time, they are confined strictly to facts, and are the result of practical experiment by myself or others, whose names I give. In all professions, and in none more so than in the practice of medicine, novel events, remarkable phases, and rare combinations are continually presenting themselves, which can only be understood and successfully encountered by the aid of general principles. Thence the need that every groom who aspires to be a successful man should have a knowledge of pathology and therapeutics, which supply the general knowledge to guide him in treating disease or complications which he has not previously experienced. From the peculiar situation of the sensitive laminæ, and their being so highly vascular and abundant in nervous texture, the disease called laminitis, which has its seat in the reticular tissue that envelopes the coffin-bone, consists, I conceive, primarily in a congestion of the blood, which is soon followed with intense inflammation ; the laminæ being situated between two hard substances, viz., the coffin-bone and the hoof, high congestive inflammation is readily produced, and the most violent pain and severe results are the consequence when inflammation ensues. Mr Percival in his " Hippopathology " has written largely upon this disease, as has also Mr Wilson, of Bradford,

and Mr Greaves, of Manchester.   Laminitis is of two
specific kinds, and may be designated natural and
unnatural.—First, natural laminitis is mostly found in
horses of a low breed, heavy and corpulent in body, such
as draught horses of various kinds, and this arises, doubtless, from constitutional causes.   Unnatural laminitis or
artificial phase of this terrible disease is most frequently
met with in light-bred animals, and no doubt is the
result of their endeavour to resist the violence occasioned
by over-exertion on hard roads, and by the exhaustion
produced by rapid driving and other artificial de-
leterious causes, such as being called upon to perform
long journeys when the stomach is overloaded with
food.   Always remember "Full feed, then rest,"—eating
large quantities of wheat or feeding upon new oats.
There is one cause, however, so prominent and influen-
tial in its character, that ought never to be lost sight
of, and that is *work* or what may be construed into
violence done to the feet ; for instance, a horse with
high stamping action going any great distance or for
any length of time upon the hard macadamised
road, or hard pavement of any kind whatever, will be
a very likely subject for an attack of this disease,
particularly if he has been idle, at rest, or unseasoned,
and is suddenly and at once put to do severe work.
It is here that the groom requires to use great
caution ; when a new horse is brought under his care
he does not know if the animal has been idle and been
"made up" for sale, and if suddenly put to hard
work the chances are he will fall to pieces.   It is a
safe plan to always put a new purchase through a

course of physic before using it. Many gentlemen turn their hunters out of condition through the summer months with the idea of resting their legs. This is a mistake for which the animal has to pay in the autumn by extra work to get it into condition again, and grooms are often put to their wits' end by the animals becoming affected with lameness in the foot as soon as they are put to work; whereas, had they been kept up during the summer months and gently exercised, their legs would have been quite fresh and their feet in good condition ; less work would have to be given to get them into hunting condition, and the owner would have sounder horses with which to commence the season, and laminitis would be known only as an ugly name. Of the former character or type of this disease many cases have come under my observation, in some of which the animals had not been out of their stables for weeks or months, and others had had only their regular work, yet all were attacked, with symptoms equally violent, with the most virulent cases that have ever come under my experience. This is one of the many evidences of the justice of my distinction of natural from unnatural or artificial phases of laminitis, and which cannot be accounted for by the general and popularly received theory that this disease is the off-spring of violence and over-work. Surely, then, my theory is not ill-founded ; there must be some occult or mysterious cause for this disease presenting itself under the peculiar circumstances I have now related. What, I have frequently asked myself, is this hidden

or undiscovered cause ?   Is it idiosyncrasy or some
peculiar element in the system of the patient?   Is it
cachexia or a bad habit of the body ? and when ru-
minating upon this subject, I have frequently had
brought to my recollection the remark of Professor
Spooner upon this form of disease, which was to the
effect that laminitis to all intents and purposes
belongs to the rheumatic class; and more lately, on
perusing a paper by Mr. Greaves, I find two right words
used in the right place in reference to the active causes
of this disease, viz., igneous element.   I feel quite
satisfied that the words "igneous element" are the
very essence of this lamentable disease of the horse,
lurking as it does in the system, waiting only for some
exciting circumstances to bring it into activity.   Nor
is it possible for the man attending upon the animals
to prevent this complaint, any more than he can
prevent himself from an attack of rheumatic fever—a
case in the human subject analogous to laminitis in
the horse.   Here we have the symptoms somewhat
similar to those we see in the laminitic acute pain—
extreme tenderness attended with great constitutional
disturbance, extreme restlessness, intense thirst, and
loss of appetite, the pulse often up to 120, and full,
hard, and jerking; the bowels obstinately costive, the
urine scanty and high coloured, with a strong acid
reaction; the skin is often bathed in a profuse sweat,
which, however, affords no relief, and it is an established
fact with the medical profession that rheumatism is
essentially a blood disease, and that the poison which
is accumulated in it appears to be lactic acid.   It also

contains a large excess of fibrine, the urine is excessively acid, high coloured, and contains much uric acid, and the remedy of the faculty in such cases is the treatment by alkalis. . . . Since the system is saturated with the acid, the most rational treatment is the alkalis, and it is the most successful—bicarbonate of potass, nitrate, bitartrate, and acetate. The symptoms of laminitis are, that the horse stands in a fixed position; if confined to the fore feet, the symptoms are of that peculiar character that they can hardly by any person of experience be mistaken, "all of a heap" is the old phrase used to denote the animal's position; the pulse is full, frequent, and remarkably hard, the respiration seeming to sympathise with the pulse. The horse places its hind feet under it in order to take the weight of its body off the fore feet. It groans and moans from the severity of the pain which in extreme cases lays it prostrate. If forced to step forward it most unwillingly does so; and its method of accomplishing it is expressive of no disease save laminitis. The feet are hot and painful; if one foot is held up, which in some cases is very difficult to do, it can scarcely stand upon the other; it does not like to get up when laid down, and if compelled, does so with great difficulty, and it is very unwilling to move from one place to another. Throbbing of the pastern arteries is another well-marked symptom. The mouth is parched, the mucus membranes vascular and scarlet in colour; parts of its body are in a state of tremor, and it is continually changing the position of its feet in search of relief. The pain is explained by a larger amount of blood to the nerves of the part, combined with the pressure of the surrounding textures upon them. It is accordingly most severe when the surroundings are the most unyielding. With increased heat of the surface, great thirst, dry skin, scanty and high-coloured urine, we have the most obstinate and sluggish state of the bowels. Many different modes of treatment have been recommended, and reasoning on general physiological principles, the functions of the alimentary canal are so tardily carried on that we cannot insure the operation of a purge under twenty-four hours, there being no animal but the horse in which acute disease makes such sad havoc in so short a space of time. Empty his stomach you cannot with an emetic, nor can you purge in a few hours; and, well knowing the obstinacy of the bowels in this disease, our measure must be prompt to act, for the grand purpose, if the groom or veterinary surgeon desires to be successful, must be to conquer the disease by resolution. As every other mode of termination is unfavourable, to bring about this issue is the aim and end of every one treating this malady, and as the nature of the disease, its seat and the disorganisation which it produces are well known, this result is not so difficult of accomplishment as at first sight appears. In proof of this I beg to offer to my readers the treatment I have found successful during a number of years' practice. It as is follows : bleeding from the coronary plexus, give aconite in ten-grain doses every hour in one pint of cold water ; gently purge, give nitrate of potass, three drachms in cold water every time the patient drinks, day and night ; give half a pound of new yeast two or three times a day; pour cold water with great force upon its feet, every hour day and night. *Bleeding:* In inflammation there is a diminished action, that is, diminished contractility of the small arteries, with increased action of the heart, and the two together keep up that dilated condition of the small vessels which is the essence of inflammation. It is obvious that there are two ways by which these small vessels may be restored to their healthy degree of contraction, the first is by lessening the quantity of blood to the part and the second by increasing the contractility. In acute inflammation both these remedies are required. If the inflammation be recent, the small vessels may recover themselves if at once relieved from the undue quantity of blood sent from the heart. In this case the abstraction of blood and using depressing remedies will suffice; but if the inflammation be chronic, the small vessels may have so lost their contractility as not to recover themselves, though the blood circulates through them in diminished quantity, and in this case such remedies must be used as will restore the lost contractility; precisely the same treatment is required as in congestion. The treatment of inflammation is two-fold. It consists in diminishing the quantity of blood sent out by the heart on the one hand, and restoring the lost contractility on the other. As increased action of the heart occurs only in acute inflammation, it is in that form alone that general remedies are required; these are blood-letting, active purgatives, and depressants. Bleeding alone, though often repeated, will not suffice to subdue inflammation, for each bleeding is followed by reaction, and that re-

action again establishes the inflammation. . . . .
By combining depletion with depressing remedies, we
save blood and avert chronic disease. The great
principle to be observed in acute inflammation is to
subdue it at once, so as not to allow reaction, and give
the small blood-vessels time to contract to their proper
size. Aconite, given in ten-grain doses in half-a-pint
of cold water every hour, diminishes the vascular and
nervous excitement after two or three doses; the
patient seems inclined to lie down and sleep, which
seems to be the desideratum so strongly urged by Mr.
Greaves—viz., get the weight off the feet. Large doses
of aconite produces alarming symptoms and considerable
excitement, but in small doses I have often seen its
sedative effects almost instantaneous. Aconite being a
most powerful medicine, should be always used with
great caution ; Fleming's tincture is by far the safest, if
it is thought advisable to give large doses. The largest
should be given first, and this must not exceed twenty
minims, in one ounce of liq. ammonia acet. and a pint of
water ; in four hours half the quantity, and in five hours
after one quarter. Over-doses of aconite are known by
a great depression, anxious countenance, accelerated
breathing, increased rapidity, and diminished volume
of the pulse, and contracted pupils. I well recollect
Professor Spooner saying that belladonna was unequalled
as a sedative, for you to have two objects in view in
administering it, it being the best sedative, and also
a laxative, which power no other sedative possesses.
Mr. Brown says of aconite that, given with caution
in small doses and well diluted, it has proved in his

experience the best sedative, and stands pre-eminent as
a diuretic. Nitrate of potass, given repeatedly in water,
possesses the property of destroying or neutralising
certain morbid poisons existing in the blood, as well as
in a less marked manner of checking inflammation,
which result is attributed, at least in part, to its well-
known property of rendering the fibrine of the blood
more soluble. In laminitis cold water should be
poured with great force upon the feet, as they are hot
and dry; it reduces the temperature, lowers the circulation and soothes the nervous system, diminishes the
extreme sensibility, and restores the contractility of
the capillary vessels, thereby preventing any further
effusion, and allowing the absorbent vessels to remove
any fluid that may have been thrown out. In this
disease the functions of the stomach and digestive
organs are either primary or sympathetically impaired,
and the assimilation of nutriment consequently very
feeble; it becomes a necessity to supply such con-
centrated forms of nutriment as will be most certain
and readily absorbed by the digestive organs. I have
often given two or three eggs in half a pint of cold
water every two hours night and day, until the fever
abates, then give mash, raw swede, mangold, carrot;
if in summer green food in small quantities, and
change its food often. Horses once having laminitis
are always liable to a relapse upon any extra exertion.
" No foot, no horse" is a proverb staunch and true;
yet when we look to the numerous complaints and
diseases of the foot that the horse is subject to, and all
the evils that arise from the ignorance and prejudice

of the shoeing smith, the groom, and the master, the wonder is, not that we have many lame horses, but that we have any sound ones. How many smiths are there who will boast that they can drive a nail its full length up the delicate hoof of the foot as they say without injuring the foot. Many, again, will use eight, and I have seen some horses with nine nails to hold one shoe, and then after doing all they can to destroy the foot they grumble and call the horse a brittle-footed brute, and tell us the horse has not a bit of foot to nail to. They do not think, and they do not like to be told, that it is their ignorance of the structure of the hoof that has been the cause of all the mischief. The fact is the nails they drive cut the fibres with which the hoof is composed, and as these fibres are cut so they become dead horn, all the nutritious mucus being cut off that supplies life and elasticity to the hoof no life really existing from the part they have in-jured up at the clenches to the line of demarcation at the sole. It is not only the fibres that are cut that receive injury, but in driving the nails the fibres are driven out of their natural course sideways, and the hoof between the nails is compressed together as if in a vice, preventing the pores of the hoof from per-forming their proper functions, hence the folly of shoeing-smiths driving so many nails into the foot. A well-fitted and well-made shoe will keep on the horse better with six nails than a bad one will with ten, yet we find many smiths are perfectly contented to nail on the horse a piece of iron bent round with rough nail holes punched in and call it a shoe; this we find often with the farm or cart horse, and you can often hear them say " That will do for him—it's only a cart horse," putting one in mind of the words of Tom Hood, " He's only a pauper, whom nobody owns." The smith does his worst for the foot of the horse with bad shoes and many nails, and the groom often helps him to complete the mischief, by using compounds of fat and tar and other substances to dress the hoof, and stopping with cow-dung to soften the feet. If I was asked " Does hoof-dressing do any good ?" I should say decidedly " No ;" for it stops the air-cells and prevents free perspiration. Does cow-dung do any good ? It enables the smith, without hard labour, to cut away that block of horn on the sole, and pare the frog into a nice shape, so that if the horse, in trotting over rough roads and loose stones, puts its foot on a stone, it becomes bruised, and may fall down and break its knees, and sometimes its owner's neck. The reader may ask, do I use hoof-dressing ? I tell them candidly " Yes," then you may well ask why do I use it ? " Because my employer likes to see it; " and with the groom as well as the smith, it is often doing things to their employer's whim, or losing his work. So much for the use of hoplemuroma and other mixtures of its class. Now, what about paring away the sole and frog? The prevalent idea of old writers was that one pair of bones are attached to a larger one by a yielding medium substance, which by stretching admits of their descent, and that another pair—the *sessanoide*—are suspended by an elastic ligament, endowed with considerable elongating properties ; that the navicular bone is pressed

G

down on to the tendon beneath it, which in its turn reposes on the frog; and lastly that the coffin-bone is slung by elastic medium bands to the inner surface of the wall of the hoof; that these bands (the *laminæ*) allow by their stretching properties for the bones to descend, to admit of which the sole of the hoof must be cut away and otherwise weakened to avoid obstruction. Can any rational man believe that this is the material to harbour in men's brains as a foundation to build a superstructure of any kind, either of normal actions or diseased conditions? No; the anatomy of the foot must be understood, from phenomena we must arrive at systems, and then we may learn pathology. Knowledge of healthy actions first, then altered states, diseases, causes, and sequences may be understood, hence the necessity of a class in the Royal Veterinary College, where the aspirant groom and smith could study and pass an examination in the anatomical structures of the horse, the foot in particular.

Such a class would go further towards a rational mode of shoeing being adopted than all the abusive works upon the groom and blacksmith ever written. Teach the blacksmith and groom first, then if they do wrong blame them, but do not blame a man for his ignorance if you do not try and teach him. It is easy to call a man a fool, but, as daft Will Perkins, of Melton Mowbray, once said, what God left out no man can put in; and depend upon it that those writers who are ever ready to call all grooms and smiths fools, only do so from being so familiar with their own names. . .
. . As I have said, bad shoeing and bad management

of the foot of the horse lead to and are the primary cause of many diseases, amongst which none are worse than navicular joint disease; and as my writings are only meant as a sort of pilot to guide the groom in his pursuit of knowledge under difficulties, I would here impress upon his mind that although I from time to time give the symptoms and treatment of different diseases, yet they are only to enable him to become a good nurse, and be the right hand of the practical veterinary surgeon ; for if the veterinary surgeon finds an intelligent groom, he will most assuredly be able to leave his medicine with confidence, and the groom should always bear in mind that practice makes perfection,—that however well versed a groom may be, the veterinary surgeon has the best of him in practice as he is enabled to see a hundred cases to the groom's one. Calling in the aid of the veterinary surgeon is not a sign of the groom's ignorance, as some are too prone to remark, but to any man of common sense, it would prove that the groom knew he had a bad case, and also that his treatment was the right one to adopt under the circumstances, and that by calling in the aid of the practical veterinary to consult with he was doing his best for the benefit of his employer. It always gives the author great pleasure to call in such men as Professor Pritchard, of London ; Mr Wadlow, of Oxford ; Mr Stanley, of Leamington ; or Mr Broad, of Bath ; to consult with in difficult cases ; they are men of knowledge and do not call grooms and blacksmiths fools, but will kindly point out the quicksands under their feet, and help them on to firm ground and sound judgment. It is owing to the friendship of those men and Mr

Gamgee, Mr Varnell, and the late Professor Dick that the author has been able to obtain knowledge, and by the advice given him by those gentleman he is enabled to pen these papers for the benefit of his less fortunate fellow-grooms, and for younger men having horses under their care.

NAVICULAR DISEASE

Is chiefly met with in the fine breeds of speedy horses, with which and in their special kind of work a more constant energetic pressure is kept up in the region of this bone. The causes of this disease, like most others, are essentially of two kinds, viz., predisposing and actual or direct causes. The first consists of the management of horses from the time they are foals to adult age. Well-formed strong feet, all other things being the same, withstand the effects of after-causes longest. Bad shoeing and fast work under weight or draught are the common exciting causes of this disease and most other diseased conditions of the foot of the horse. Bad shoeing is a vague expression, but I call all bad in degree that is not done by system, subordinate to the necessary knowledge of the foot. There are some bad habits which have found their way into the shoeing shop, and which it is almost impossible to obliterate from the mind of the smith; amongst which none are worse than paring the frog and sole; weakening the wall of the foot with the rasp, and softening the foot with any mixture should also be avoided. As no skill is needed in attending to this step, alike conservative and remedial in tendency, I submit it with recommendation that it be taken as a rule applicable to all classes of horses. Navicular disease never occurs suddenly, is never caused by bruises from stones as alleged, nor does it appear as a primary affection. The coffin-bone having the whole weight and exertion to sustain is always the first to suffer, and it is when an alteration from the normal state takes place in the coffin-bone and the other component structures of the foot, that derangement of functions and stress of pressure is imposed upon the navicular bone. The coffin-bone undergoes more change in physical formation and far more rapidly than occurs in other bones, I may say of any animal, for the reason that no bone is placed under so many complications of influence and misapplied art and exertion combined. The *semilunæ* crest and the normal asperities of the coffin-bone become absorbed under the influence prevalent by which the attacking processes for the tendon, the planta band and the frog, are all weakened and their positions become altered. The navicular-bone is more and more called upon to bear pressure when its normal bulk would lack space, therefore absorption of its substance takes place from within, until at length the outer surface breaks down ; being always on its lower and posterior surface where the ulcerated apertures one or more are seen, whence lymph issuing becomes attached to the tendon, by which effort of nature the structure becomes in some measure fixed together, and the otherwise unsupportable friction is diminished. For the treatment of this disease I repeat the words of Professor Gamgee, in a lecture upon this subject delivered by him at the New College of Veterinary

Surgeons.   He said, " Our treatment is all of a
prophylactic kind ; firstly preventive measures are the
great resource, the taking care of the stable ere the steed
is lost is our watchword; but cases will make their
appearance, and although not one case in ten of those
pronounced to be navicular disease are of that type, yet
in various stages of progress cases of the navicular disease
frequently appear.   My remedies," said the Professor, " in
these cases consist in taking very much the same
measure as I adopt for the prevention or rather the
maintenance of healthy action regardless of any particular
disease.   I remove causes, *i.e.*, in the first place the shoes
and withdraw all ascertainable causes of pain as soon as
possible ; rest and some fomentation to the feet are
amongst the most effective means.   Continued rest in a
loose box for two or three weeks may be necessary, during
which time the feet will acquire form and strength from
the treatment I carry out, viz., no softening application
after the first two or three days when circulation of the
blood will have found its equilibrium over the foot, after
which cleanliness and care, and abstaining from
debilitating the hoof is observed.   But we may say this
is not surgery ; would you not blister, bleed, insert setons,
and if lameness continued persistent unnerve the horse ?
I shake my head and say—No.   It is not pretended that
I can cure all cases submitted to me of the character,
under notice.   Then what is to be done with the
incurables ? are they not to be submitted to the ordinary
routine of successive operations ? I can hardly be made
to reply ; and for the following reasons.   I saw so much
of what is called the surgery of these cases in my early

days, such torture, butchery, and sacrifice of property, that I tried what I believed then the most rational mode of procedure, and have been rewarded with great success. The few cases of protracted and advanced disease, which after due observation and trial I diagnose as incurable, I advise to be put out of their miserable state." Such is the opinion of Professor Gamgee upon this terrible disease. We have still yet another complaint of the feet of the horse, and though it has but a simple name, yet it is a painful and troublesome disease. I am speaking of

CORNS,

And those of my readers who are troubled with them can sympathise with the horse when it is afflicted with corns. This disease in the foot of the horse has acquired a name which but ill expresses its nature. It bears but little affinity to corns of the human foot ; instead of being hard as in the human subject they are thin and very weak, and caused by pressure on the sole at the angle of the bars of the feet, the horn becomes more spongy and soft than at other parts, and it is so sensitive that upon the slightest pressure the horse indicates that he feels pain. When the foot becomes contracted, that portion of the sole intervening between the external crust which is wiring in, and the bars which oppose that con- traction are squeezed very severely, which induces inflam- mation, and hence it is that feet that are contracted are almost always subjects that are afflicted with corns. The effects of this pressure induce a small quantity of extravasated blood, and the horn being secreted in less quantities and being more spongy it has a tendency to inclose in it a portion of this extravasated blood. Another, and the most common cause of corns, is allowing the shoes to remain too long on the horse's feet; nothing is more injurious than to allow a shoe to remain too long on the foot, yet many owners of horses, to save a few shillings per year, will let the shoes remain on the horse for six weeks and two months at a stretch, at the risk of producing corns, and spraining the back sinews by an extra amount of leverage caused by the lengthened growth of the toe. The shoe remaining on too long is sure to become embedded in the heel of the foot, consequently the hoof grows down on the outside of the shoe and the bearing is thus thrown on to the angular portion of the sole. Continual pressure on the sole is sure to induce inflammation and corns, the shoe being on a long time gets loosened at the heels, which admits of gravel between it and the crust, which having accumulated at the angles naturally insinuates itself into the heels and produces a sore. As I said before, nothing can be more injudicious than to allow the shoes to remain too long on; even if they are not worn out they should be taken off every twenty-one days and re-adjusted to free the feet from long continued pressure. In shoeing, too, the blacksmith will often resort to that injurious and ridiculous cutting and shaping of the foot, and cutting away the bars. This renders it necessary that the shoe should be levelled inward, so as to accommodate it to their senseless cutting and shaping of the foot; consequently an unnatural disposition to contraction is induced by this slanting inward direction of the shoe. There can be but little doubt but corns are mainly owing to the faults of shoeing, as well as to the fact of shoeing itself, however well performed, preventing the due expansion of the horn when the sole is growing downward. The treatment of this disease, like all others and the diseases of the foot in particular, must be begun by removing the cause. The first thing to do with a corn is to remove the shoe and pare out the corn ; do not cut the bars or heels ; pare the corn until it will bend under the pressure of the finger. Veterinary surgeons adopt different modes of treatment of corns, but the writer, having after many experiments adopted the following with great success, sometimes from continual pressure upon the heels by a bad-made shoe, or by neglect in not having the horse's shoes taken off at proper intervals, the corn, or the foot between the horn of the heel and the bars, will become festered ; if in paring out the corn matter is observed, open the sole to allow of free suppuration, then poultice the foot with warm linseed meal for two or three days ; after the suppuration has ceased dip a piece of cotton wool into carbolised oil (strength five parts oil to one of acid), and insert it into the hole in the foot ; in a few days the foot will have become sound, and by good shoeing and care the corn will cease to trouble, as we have set up a healthy reaction of the food. If the corn is only of the ordinary kind, after the horn has been pared away, hold up the foot and pour a small quantity of muriatic acid upon the corn, keep the foot up until the acid has ceased to hiss, then have the shoe put on, but mind it has a fair and level bearing and broad enough at the heel to cover the point of the bar at its juncture with the heel. Never allow the smith to spring the heel, as they say " to take the pressure off the heel," for by so doing they avoid one trouble and cause two. If the shoe is sprung at the heel there is no level bearing, and great leverage is given to the shoe which unduly bears upon the quarters of the foot, the quarters being the weakest part of the foot it is easily injured, and thus to avoid a corn we do our best to set up inflammation. Another evil is, that by an uneven bearing and great leverage we put too much strain on the nails, causing them to break and loosen the shoe. In cases of bad corns, if you want the pressure taken off the heel, make the smith thin out the heel of the shoe to one half the substance of the shoe for about one inch and a quarter from the point of the heel; this should be done on the wearing surface next the ground, and upon no account on the side next the foot. If these instructions are fully carried out, the author is confident that the worst corns can be cured in twice or three times shoeing, much annoyance to master and man saved, and relief given to the poor horse. This being a disease brought on entirely by man's ignorance, stupidity, and neglect, it is time we turned our attention to the subject, and by careful shoeing and common sense to atone for the suffering of the past, by studying the comfort of the horse in the future.

THRUSH

Is another disease of the foot of the horse, which, however much veterinary surgeons and other writers may say to the contrary, the author is satisfied is mainly caused by man's neglect. It is a disease that is observed in horses of all ages, the colt in the farm-yard and the old and worn-out carriage horse. Thrush in the foot of the colt is produced by pressure and contraction of the quarters, which is thereby diminished in size, and the lower portion of the fleshy or sensitive frog being confined is irritated and inflamed, which induces ulceration, and when matured is manifested by matter being discharged from the cleft of the frog. The cause of this contraction is attributable to neglect in not having the colt's feet examined regularly, and the heels rasped down and the toe shortened. We never see thrush in the foot of a thorough-bred colt, from the simple reason that their feet are not neglected. It would not pay, for who would give four or five hundred guineas for a thorough-bred colt, however good-looking he may be, if his feet were rotten with thrush? If neglect will not pay in the race-horse, neither will it do so in the hackney, carriage, or cart horse, yet many farmers and owners of young horses will risk contracting thrush and numerous other diseases of the foot for the sake of saving a few shillings;—and few indeed it is, for the foot if looked to once a month would become sound and well formed, instead of weak, diseased, and malformed. During the stage of inflammation the lower surface of the sensible frog, secretes pus, instead of the horny substance which is

its proper function. When a frog is in a healthy condition the cleft sinks but a small way into the foot;
contraction, however, or any other disease, often
affects the cleft so that it extends in length and often
penetrates deep into the sensitive frog, and it is
through this deep and diseased fissure that the matter
from the thrush discharges itself. Any complaint
which affects the healthy condition of the foot will
induce thrush, which, differing from most diseases of
the foot, is mostly the worst in the hind feet, especially
in horses kept in the stable. This can be accounted
for by uncleanliness and bad stable management, and
that the hind feet are subject to the baneful effects of
being immersed in the dung and urine, producing
irritation and generating disease. Besides the hind
feet are farther removed from the centre of circulation
than the fore feet, which consequently subjects them
to an accumulation of matter and grease, as well as
other affections to which they are liable. Contraction
is generally the cause of thrush in the fore feet, and
contraction is caused chiefly by bad shoeing and neglect of the foot of the unshod colt, therefore I contend
that I am within bounds when I assert that thrush is
caused by man's neglect. A horse may have thrush
without being lame, as it often happens that no
alteration whatever is to be seen on the foot thus
diseased, and it may require a close inspection to
detect that it is diseased, but it will always be
manifested by the disagreeable smell that invariably
accompanies this complaint. In some cases no tenderness of the frog attends thrush, and the horse

would be considered legally sound. This, however, seems strange, as a horse with thrush may, and indeed is likely to assume a worse aspect, particularly if not remedied in time, and hence it may lead to positive unsoundness. The remedies of this complaint are undoubtedly by astringents. The foot should be pared of all the loose and rotten horn, then cut away the diseased portion, wash with warm water strong with soda, after which it may be dressed every day with the following put on a pledget of tow:—Blue vitriol two ounces, white vitriol one ounce, tar one pound, hog's-lard one pound. The vitriols to be finely powdered and mixed with the lard and tar, or instead of the former carbolised oil may be used with good effect. It is not judicious to stop the running of thrush quickly, as by so doing the humour may ascend to the heels and leave the animal with bad heels and swelled legs. During the treatment of thrush the horse's feet should be kept dry and clean.

SEEDY TOE

Is another disagreeable and ofttimes troublesome complaint. Seedy toe and its companion canker are to all intents and purposes one disease, only having different situations in the foot. This complaint is met with in horses of all ages, and mostly in well-bred horses. There is a wasting or decay of the fibres of the hoof, between the outside horn and the sensitive lamilla of the foot, often becoming hollow up to near the coronary ring. Horses that have been lying in fields of damp black vegetable soil are the most subject to seedy toe, and others that are turned into a dung-yard upon hot dung will become affected. Many writers say that seedy toe is caused by the shoeing smith putting the hot shoe upon the horse's foot to burn it to a level bed, thereby depriving the horn of its natural elasticity. I have never seen a case of seedy toe that I could trace to that cause, and am of opinion that we must look to other sources for the true cause. After numerous experiments, I have come to the conclusion that seedy toe is, if I may use the term, a vegetable disease, being caused by moisture fostering the growth of a minute kind of fungus, which lives upon the horn, just as dry rot is caused by a fungus living upon the wood. Having arrived at that conclusion, I have always resorted to the following treatment, and never had a case that did not succumb after twice or thrice dressing. First take a small searching knife and cut away all the rotten horn as far as you can between the sole and crust; cut away the crust to prevent it breaking, then pour into the affected part carbolic acid one part, sweet oil three parts, dip a piece of tow into the oil, and fill the hole with it, then put on the shoe, and in two or three times dressing the foot will have become sound. I had a patient last summer, an ass, which had its hoofs entirely eaten away with disease of the seedy toe type. I dressed its feet firstly with pure carbolic acid, the next day I dressed them with carbolised oil, filling the space between the little outside horn it had left with tow, and turned it out into the field. In twice dressing I had killed the fungus, and now its feet are perfectly sound. Perhaps some of my readers who have seedy toe among their horses, will place a portion of the bad hoof under a powerful microscope, and ascertain if my theory as to fungus is correct; but, let it be fungus or what it may, it cannot stand carbolic acid. My reason for first trying the acid was that it possesses the power to prevent decomposition and destroying minute animal and vegetable organism. Perhaps other substances possessing similar properties may be as effective in seedy toe, but the writer, being satisfied that he can cure every case of seedy toe that comes under his care with carbolic acid, is quite content with it without further experiment.

CANKER,

Unlike seedy toe, is mostly met with in the low breed of horses, heavy cart and dray horses being most subject to it. By some writers it is considered of an hereditary nature, but I am inclined to look upon it as upon thrush, which is in itself almost always the true cause of canker; and as thrush is the offspring of neglect of the foot and bad shoeing, so is canker the offspring of a neglected thrush; or, I may say, thrush is the primary cause, and canker the secondary. Still there are cases where the canker is caused by puncture, bruise, corn, or quittor, yet it is mostly thrush that is its primary cause. Canker consists of a separation of the horny substance from the sensible fleshy and bony portion of the foot, caused by the growth of fungus matter shooting up and occupying parts of, or the entire sole of the foot and frog. The cause of this disease, like many others incidental to the cart horse, is negligence in the master and groom and the shoeing smith combined. The chief cause of canker is produced by ponderous heavy shoes with which they are shod, and the large nails with which they are necessarily attached to the foot; these produce contraction, which produces thrush, and thrush produces canker. Thus neglect is the primary cause of nine-tenths of the so-called hereditary diseases of the foot. The dirty state of the stables and the neglect of the feet are a fertile source of this complaint. Cleanliness and attention to the horse's feet are a preventive which is far before all known methods of cure. When once this disease has been induced it is extremely difficult to cure, and it is advisable to call in the aid of the veterinary surgeon. Although I have found the same treatment I adopt for seedy toe to be very effectual, I will here quote a few words from Mr Brown upon this disease. He says, "Besides the hereditary predisposition of work-horses to canker, in order to give them foothold it becomes necessary to raise the heels of the hind feet so much that all pressure on the frog is done away with, which has the effect of destroying its functions, and consequently rendering it liable to disease." This is most erroneous, for I contend it is not necessary to put heavy shoes on the cart horse, neither is it necessary to put on large caulkings to give him a foot-hold; the animal has a far better foot-hold if shod plain with his frog on the ground, to allow that natural wedge to take the place that nature evidently intended it for, *i.e.,* the expansion of the foot, and to prevent the horse slipping.

The American farmer does not have his horses shod upon the absurd principle of high caulkings as we find them in this country, yet their horses have as heavy loads to draw and as steep hills to climb. They study their horse's comfort much more than is done by the farmers and carters of this boasted Christian land. How much straining, fear, torture, and misery, would be taken away from the poor horse if brains were more plentiful in men! By the very simple contrivance of brake-power to every cart, the horse could go as easily down a steep hill as on the level road. I have seen such a contrivance in Scotland upon the carts drawing stone from quarries. It is simply a piece of wood attached to the after-part of the cart with two short pieces of chain; in the centre of the wood a small rod of iron passes through to the axletree to which it is attached, on the end which projects through the wood a screw-handle is attached, with which the carter can screw the block of wood so that it has a bearing upon both wheels. The contrivance is very simple and the cost trifling, as any country smith could make it and put it on, and the saving in wear and tear of horse flesh must be enormous. This simple break would be far superior to the skid pan and chain upon our waggons, as the power is upon both wheels at once, and the pressure can be put on without the horses being stopped and can be taken off without backing the load. If owners of waggons and carts would have them put on, their carters would soon appreciate them; for as a rule they are very fond of their horses, especially if the farmer does not half-starve them. The late Mr Mechi used to jocularly say that "the ploughmen were more fond of their horses than their wives; they love to see them fat, with skins as glossy as

H

velvet and as sleek as moles." No man knew more about the ploughman than he, or was more beloved by (to use his own words) his old and trusted servants, many of whom had worked for him for twenty years and upwards; one of his great secrets of successful farming was to get good men and keep them. He studied the welfare of his men, and his men repaid him by faithfully doing their duty, and loving and caring for his horses and stock, because he loved and cared for them.

I now come to another troublesome complaint of the foot. Ah! how many are there who can tell? only the man with large studs under his care. The diseases, modifications, and complications are truly amazing and fearful to contemplate. Who will say that

SANDCRACK

is not as bad as any other disease of the foot, and quite as painful to the animal? Who of my readers has torn the nail of his finger down to the quick, and experienced the pain when he has touched anything with the injured finger? He at least will know something of the pain the poor horse has to suffer when his feet are afflicted with sandcrack. Sandcrack is a disease that is mostly met with in horses working upon hard roads and drawing heavy loads. In the cart horse it is chiefly found in the hind feet, but in the lighter breed of horses it is mostly confined to the fore feet. Sandcrack is simply a bursting of the horny matrix that holds together the horn fibres or horn tubes of the hoof. It may only reach to a very limited extent at the coronet, or it may extend from the coronet to the ground surface. It may come on gradually, or it may come on suddenly. When it comes on suddenly it is attended with great suffering. Occasionally we have suppuration in the fissure, sloughing of the laminæ, caries of the bone, superfluous granulation, and in very severe cases the animal gives up, refuses all food, sinks, and dies. Mr. Greaves, in a letter in the *Veterinarian*, vol. 48, p. 72, says, " I fully believe that in many cases there is a constitutional tendency to sandcrack, for if we get the fissure to grow out and entirely disappear in one place another crack will make its appearance in another part of the hoof. We often notice that the horse with a sandcrack in one foot, whether it be hind or fore, will sooner or later have another sandcrack in one of the other feet." The author cannot fall into the view of Mr. Greaves upon the constitutional point of the disease, unless, indeed, the patient has an hereditary malformation of the foot, as some horses have. Colts by Snowstorm, for instance, have most of them one club foot. I am more in favour of the view taken by my friend Mr. Broad, of Bath. In a conversation I once had with him about this disease, he said, " The majority of cases of sandcrack that came under his notice for treatment were those that occur in the toes of heavy cart horses; they do not arise as the effects of dryness or the defects of the horn itself, as, on the contrary, they occur in the strongest and thickest of hoofs which are defective in shape, being mostly very upright, so that when the horse is shod with high caulkings—the principal cause—and put to excessively heavy pulling, the front part of the hoof gets more strain upon it than it can sustain, the result being a fracture of the horn.

High caulkings, and indeed caulkings of any kind, are a curse to the horse, and until a class is opened for instructing the blacksmith in the fundamental principles of the foot, the absurd, foolish, and ridiculous system of shoeing will not improve. The old smiths will tell us that they have shod horses upon that principle all their lives, and their fathers did so before them, so they must know; and they instil this doctrine into their apprentices, and after they have served their time they in their turn become as pig-headed as their teacher, and strongly opposed to any alteration of the system. The man who dares to assert that there can and ought to be improvements made is considered a raving lunatic. The treatment I have always adopted in sandcrack is that which was recommended to me by Mr. Broad, of Bath, and his brother in London. If my patient is lame I immediately put on a bar-shoe. A bar-shoe is a round shoe, not a common shoe made of bar-iron, fitted full at the toe with a clip on each side, but having no bearing opposite the crack. The shoe is fitted long, and made thin at the heel, the object being to enable the horse to bear his weight on the heels, which he can do better in this shaped shoe than any other, or indeed even without a shoe, at the same time applying plenty of cold water to the coronet. Nothing will make the horn grow so fast as plenty of cold water. Some people order poultices, but they are difficult to keep on; holes are sure to wear through the bag, the poultice falls through, and the foot becoming dry, they do more harm than good. Give physic, and in nine cases out of ten the patient in a few days is free from lameness. I then adopt a practice recommended by Mr. Broad, of Star-street, Edgware-road, London, upwards of thirty years ago, and practised by him and his brother at Bath with success up to the present time. It consists in cutting a notch with a drawing-knife, about half an inch from each side of the crack as near the coronet as possible, and about a quarter of an inch deep, sufficiently large to allow the embedding of the head of small horse nails. If the crack is long, cut two others an inch lower down, then have a nail prepared in the ordinary way, with the exception that they are pointed on the reverse side to prevent punctur-ing the quick, a case of which I never had. Never make a hole with a pricker or bore it with a redhot wire. Before using, the nails are put into a vice and the head hammered to form a shoulder, to prevent it being driven too far into the wall and breaking out the hold. After being driven carefully through the notches, a long clinch is left, the crack is then drawn closely together with the pincers, and all made smooth with the rasp to prevent the nails being trodden out. Then with the use of the bar-shoe, and a constant application of cold water with a linen bandage round the coronet, the hoof will soon grow sound, and in course of time grow out. Before quitting the subject of diseases of the foot of the horse, there is yet one more, no better than the others I have described, but, if possible, it is worse. Those of my readers who have had the misfortune to have a horse lame with

QUITTOR

will be able to endorse my remarks, as no man is anxious to have a second case after experiencing the

first.   A wound of the coronet, whether it proceeds
from a tread or otherwise, should be carefully and immediately attended to, because if sand or gravel get into
the wound it is likely to produce those deep-seated
ulcerations that are termed pipes or sinuses, which
constitute the disease called quittor.   It may also
proceed from any wound of the foot, and in any part of
it.   In all ulcers matter is secreted, and the part affected
cannot possibly heal until the matter is discharged.   In
wounds of the foot there is much difficulty in the matter
proceeding from ulceration finding its way from under
the hoof, which covers the foot with its various complicated parts.   The consequence is, it accumulates under
the hoof until it has increased to such an extent that it
must find an escape in some way, and frequently forces
itself out in all directions, separating the little fleshy
plates from their connexion with the horny ones of the
crust, or disuniting the fleshy sole from the horny one,
and in extreme cases eats its way deeply into the internal
parts of the foot, forming pipes and sinuses, which run in
all directions.   If quittor arises from a wound in the
lower portion of the foot, the matter which is collected
in it after the ulcer has ripened, being confined there,
issues from it, and induces a separation between the
horny and fleshy sole, and having accumulated in considerable quantities, at length discharges itself at the
coronet, generally close to the quarter.   This, however,
does not manifest itself to any extent, as both the
aperture and quantity of matter that oozes out are
apparently so insignificant that they would lead an inexperienced person to suppose the discharge of little

consequence. In this, however, they will be sadly mistaken, for the most serious mischief lurks within, and the difficulty of removing it is extremely great. In this state of the disease, although the fistula is of very small dimensions, the effect of this confined matter will have extended almost all over the entire quarter, and the horny sole may be separated from the foot. The matter may have penetrated and lodged beneath the ligaments and cartilages of the coffin-joint; and besides the pressure of the matter, wherever it has forced its way to, will have formed ulcerations which are most difficult to heal, and the horn which has been separated from the sensible parts below will never unite with them again, thus producing an evil of the worst description. Quittor often proceeds from neglected bruises and injuries to the sole of the foot. When horses have flat feet, and are ridden over a rough, uneven, stony road, the feet are very liable to be injured, and especially by getting a small stone under a shoe, between it and the sole where broad web shoes are used, to give what the smith calls "cover" to the sole, which he has pared away, leaving only the sixth of an inch of horn on the sole to protect it against stones, so that the poor animal cannot step upon a stone without seriously bruising the foot. Animals also shod with the broad web shoe are much more likely to get stones fast between the frog and the shoe, and are by some men driven long journeys with a stone in the shoe, because they either do not see it or are too lazy to get down and take it out. When narrow web shoes are used, we are told by the smith that the horse is sure to hurt its feet on the stones, as they have no cover to the sole. In this instance they are strictly true, for they, by a free use of the knife, have taken away all the true cover with which Nature had fortified the foot, seeing the nature of the work the horse was destined to fulfil. If the horse is shod with narrow web shoes, and the smith forbidden to touch the sole or frog with the knife, the horse will be much less liable to receive injuries from treading upon stones, as the shoe is less liable to pick them up, and Nature has herself put a protection on the sole to prevent injury of a far superior material to any of man's invention. It must be evident that this is a case which can only be successfully treated by a veterinary surgeon or a man well versed in the superstructure of the foot. In most instances it becomes necessary to cut away the greater portion of the horny sole of the foot, and thereafter to restore the healthy state of the tender surfaces beneath. When this has been effected the horn will be quickly reproduced, but when much of the horn of the sole has had to be cut away, it will take at least six months to restore fully that which had been removed so that the horse may be again fit to work. To restore the healthy condition of the foot very active means must be adopted; caustic applications alone will destroy the ulcerated surface. To ascertain the state of the disease a probe must be used, and if it touches any of the bones it is doubtful if a cure can be effected even by the most skilful. One thing is certain, if it is found when the probe is inserted into the fistulous openings on the coronet that the direction of the sinuses is backward, it is highly probable that a cure may be effected ; but if the pipes have a forward direction there is great doubt of a cure being effected. The treatment I have always adopted with quittors is to open the hoof in the diseased part, and allow of free suppuration ; wash clean with warm soda and water, dress, and inject into the pipes carbolised oil, strength four oil, one acid ; this requires to be done three times each day. Carbolic acid, being a powerful caustic and an antiseptic, has the power of destroying the ulceration, and its antiseptic properties prevent suppuration. In most cases of quittor after carbolic acid has wrought its work in the healing process, we often find a superflous growth of flesh, and it becomes necessary to apply nitrate of silver to remove it. This must be used with great caution, as it is of the utmost importance in this stage to check the superfluous growth without retarding the consolidating and healing process, and this cannot be done without a knowledge of the fundamental principles of the foot ; therefore it is of the utmost importance to call in the aid of the veterinary surgeon in this disease.

Before leaving the foot of the horse it will be well to consider how our horses are shod, the kind of shoes that are used, and the class of men who make them ; whether they are the shoes best adapted for the comfort and profitable working of the various kinds of horses, and if any improvement is possible to be made, for if a good system of shoeing is universally adopted we shall have given the death-blow to nine-tenths of the diseases of the foot of the horse, and the groom's millennium will have arrived. It is a generally acknowledged fact that large numbers of horses' legs and feet are worn out before the animals have arived at a mature age, and it has almost become a proverb that one horse could wear out three sets of legs. This is a very unsatisfactory state of things, the more so as nine-tenths of the diseases of the foot of the horse are the result of bad management in youth, and ignorance and neglect in after-life. Nor is this to be wondered at when we consider who our shoeing-smiths are, and the qualifications that are considered necessary for a man to shoe a horse. I do not think that I shall exceed the truth when I say, that hundreds of men are working in large shops as shoeing-smiths, who know nothing about the structure of the horse's foot. When we look to the rotten system in our army of making shoeing-smiths of tailors, plasterers, and bricklayers, labourers, is it any wonder that our shops are overrun with the so-called " shoeing-smith ? " Mr. Douglas says, " In my own regiment (the 10th Hussars), just before they went to India, out of fifteen farrier-sergeants and shoeing-smiths, there were only the farrier-major and two others who had been farriers before they joined the army. One of the twelve had been a tailor, and as such had worked in the regiment, a second had been a collier, a third a haberdasher, the fourth a groom, and the remainder clodhoppers." The writer is able to prove that the 10th Hussars is not the only regiment in the same fix; indeed, the Scots Greys and the Household Brigade a few years ago were in equally as bad a state. Yet these are the men who are held up to our eyes as pattern smiths. Go into the large shoeing establishments in London, Manchester, Nottingham, &c., and enquire of the men and their employers, and you will find that the principal recommendation of half their men is that they were farriers in our army, and being so, must understand their business. From these large shops emanate from time to time libels upon their brother Vulcans, the country shoeing-smiths, who are held up to ridicule by the gentlemen of large shops in town, where they are under the hallowed protection of having served in the army, and their employers have tacked to their names M.R.C.V.S., which may be literally read, " makers of rough, coarse, vexatious shoes." The writer's experience has led him to the conclusion that if you wanted your horses well shod, and thought of taking them to these large shops, and asked his advice upon them, he would give you the same advice that *Punch* gave to the young man about getting married, " Don't." As a general rule, these large firms turn out the worst work ; they do not take time enough to fit the shoes, but cut and rasp the foot to fit the shoe. In justice to the village smith, he, as a rule, will shoe the gentleman's horse better than at the large shops in town. If he has my lord's or the squire's horses to shoe, he is looked upon by the villagers as a man of great skill, and he devotes much time and labour to shoeing them, knowing that if they are not shod well he will in all probability lose most of the work in the village, as where the squire's horse goes the farmer follows ; and, radical though it may appear, yet the writer can positively assert that the best shoeing-smiths he has met with in England had been in the village smithy, and men who could not boast of a military training, but brought sound common sense to bear upon their work.

Now we come to the much-vexed question of what is the best system of shoeing our horses. The writer does not advocate one system more than another, but will try and point out the faults in most of them, and, contrary to most writers, will begin with the cart horse first, because he is the worst shod, unless it is indeed the blacksmith's own horse. What class of shoe is best adapted for the ordinary use of the farm horse? Most smiths and farmers like putting on heavy wide-web shoes—the farmer, from the belief that the heavy shoe has most wear; and the smith, who generally contracts for farm horses by the year, thinks that the more iron he puts on the horse, the less times he will have to shoe him during the year. This is a system void of economy, both to the shoeing-smith and farmer, as proof is not wanting that the narrow-web light shoe will wear longer and the horse will go easier than with broad heavy shoes. Mr. Douglas some years ago tried the experiment of shoeing the heavy van horses of one of the London railway companies with light narrow shoes. He took off one horse a set of shoes that after they were worn out weighed 7lb. 14oz , and put a set of new narrow-web shoes on the same horse which only weighed 7lb. 4oz., or 10ozs. less than the old worn-out shoes. The horse was put to the same work, with a result that the new narrow-web shoes wore four weeks and two days, and the broad heavy shoes only wore three weeks and four days. Mr. Douglas did not know what was the weight of the old shoes when put upon the horse, but it is only reasonable to think they would weigh 16 lb. the set, as they would no doubt be half worn away before they were termed worn out. Nor was this all; the horse did not slip half as much with the narrow shoe, and it entirely altered the horse's action. With the heavy shoe, he drove his feet along the road; with the light ones, he lifted his feet free from the ground, and put them down evenly and firmly. The author has had many cart horses shod for farm purposes, and found that if a horse with a foot $6\frac{1}{2}$ in. across was shod with shoes weighing 5 lb. the set of four shoes, they would last as long as any shoe ought to be kept on, and in many instances where the horses have been working on the land they would be good enough to remove after a month's work. This is proof that heavy shoes are more expensive than the narrow-web, light shoe, and it is false economy to load horses' feet with iron. The carriage horse requires for its work a different kind of shoe, yet whether the horse is shod for cart, carriage, or hacking, the one principle should rule all, viz., lightness of shoe, with true, even bearing upon the wall of the foot; as few nails as possible should be used, and each shoe made to fit the foot, not the foot to fit the shoe. Upwards of forty kinds of shoes have been made from time to time, each possessing some real or imaginary advantage, many of them being good, and one in particular, called the "Goodenough," which is good enough to lame half the horses with its ponderous weight and softness of metal. Another shoe has been before the public from time to time during the last twenty years, named the "Charlier," after Mons. Charlier, the inventor of that system of shoeing. It has many advantages over the old-fashioned shoe, but it again has

its drawbacks; it is a shoe that cannot be adapted to
every class of foot, and above all other class of shoe
requires great skill, care, and patience to fit and put on
with success. No smith, however skilful he may be at
the forge, can succeed with the "Charlier" shoe unless
he has a knowledge of the fundamental principles of the
structure of the horse's foot. The foot itself requires
much time before it becomes again naturalised after it
has been under a course of barbarous shoeing with the
cutting, paring, and rasping so often practised in the
shoeing-shop; and before the horse can be safely shod
with the "Charlier" the feet must be allowed time
to grow, and the sole and frog must on no account
be touched with the knife, the principle of the "Charlier"
shoe being to insert a narrow rim of iron round the wall
of the foot to prevent its breaking away, and leave all
the remainder of the foot as God formed it. If the
unshod colt is shod in this way from the first it can
do any kind of work over the roughest roads with
ease and safety, and the writer is of opinion that that
is the right time to begin with the "Charlier" shoe.
As it is with the faults of shoes and shoeing I am
dealing, I may here state that the two objections I
have found to the "Charlier" shoes is the difficulty
of getting them shod properly, and the fact that they
require a long time before the horse's feet become
naturalised. Another fault I have found in hunting
with them is that the horse cannot grip a bank. The
Toe Tip in many respects is like the "Charlier" shoe,
and is a plate of iron about five inches long and
three-quarters of an inch wide, and has generally a

clip at the toe which is put upon the horse with only four nails; the foot is lowered at the bed of the shoe and the toe shortened; the sole and frog are never touched with the knife. The lowering of the sole at the bed of the shoe is to bring the surface of the shoe flush with the sole, so that the animal has a level bearing upon the whole of its foot, and brings it as near to its natural formation as possible. This system of shoeing with tips has all the advantages of the "Charlier" without its drawbacks; they can be made and put on by any smith of ordinary skill, and there is not the danger of drawing the shoe too close to the sensitive lamillæ and setting up inflammation. That horses can do ordinary work in them is certain, and horses shod with the "Charlier" or tips are seldom known to sprain their back sinews, and never become afflicted with navicular disease. The horses of one of the coaches running from the White Horse Cellar used to be shod with tips, and many gentlemen use them exclusively for horses for all purposes, yet in the hunting field they have the same fault as the "Charlier"—want of grip at a bank. Of the ordinary hunting shoe I need scarcely speak, as it is a given fact that they require to be light, made short with the heels bevelled to prevent them being torn off when jumping into deep land. The hind shoe of the hunter should always be rounded at the toe both inside and outside, to prevent the horse cutting its heels off should he over-reach. Many horses injure themselves when running, which is called cutting, or brushing. Many methods are resorted to to prevent its occurrence, but in nine cases out of ten the horse always cuts worse in new

shoes ; indeed many horses that are habitual cutters never
cut themselves when the shoe is worn out. With horses
of this habit there is one general rule which is very
difficult to get the smith to follow, *i.e.*, get the smith to
make a shoe like the worn-out one, let him place a piece
of iron the thickness of a shoe on the inside of the
old worn-out shoe, and then he has a pattern of a new
shoe that the horse can go comfortably in. He will find
that the nearer he makes the new shoe to the shape of
the old worn-out one (upon the ground surface) the less
the horse will cut. This rule is applicable to all horses
of all gaits of going, and especially with trippers or
stumblers. The feather-edge shoe is largely used for
horses with a close gait of action with their hind legs ;
they are intended to throw the weight of the horse more
on the outer splint bone, thereby causing a wider gait of
action, yet we find many smiths who are but imperfectly
acquainted with their business will make a feather-edge
shoe, and absurdly make a caulking upon the outside
heel to bring it to a level with the hammered-up inside
feather-edge, and they are surprised to find that the horse
cuts or bruises as bad as before. If they had left the
heel on the outside the same thickness as the shoe from
the toe, they would have made, by the propping up of
the inside with a feather-edge, the horse have a wider
gait, and thereby prevented its cutting. The seated shoe
is the best of the common class of use for roadsters and
hackneys, and it is but seldom that we see one well
made. The seating of the shoe is generally unlevel, with
the outer edge the highest, whereas the seated shoe should
be of an equal thickness from toe to heel, perfectly flat

and parallel, only varying in width according to the formation of the hoof to which it is to be applied, and similar to the ordinary shoe in the fullering. The foot surface, however, differs in having a narrow plain rim about the same width as the thickness of the crust, extending round the edge of the shoe, except at the heel, where it presents a flat surface, to the extent of an inch ; the other part of the shoe is hollowed out, bevelling from the inner edge of the seat, making it thin except at the heel, which is the same thickness throughout, the intention being that the crust of the foot should bear upon and be supported by the seat of the shoe. The advantage of this shoe over the ordinary one is that of the crust resting on a flat surface instead of on an inclined plane, and as it bears on the edge it is less liable to induce contraction. The heel of the shoe should have a fair bearing upon the heel and bars of the foot. The bars should upon no account be cut away. Almost all smiths have a fancy for opening the heels, from the idea that it does good by rendering the foot neater, which is a complete fallacy, as they ought seldom or never to be touched ; as I have already shown in my description of the anatomy of the foot, the bars are the only check in preventing contraction. Nothing, therefore, should be removed but the ragged and detached portions. . . . It is intended that the shoe should rest partly on the heel and partly on the bar of the foot, consequently the bars should be allowed to remain nearly in its original condition from its first inflection, and extending down to the frog. From what we have shown it will be sufficiently evident that some skill is required to make this shoe, and properly fit and put on, yet no skill is required to cut and pare the horse's foot, that being a part of the smith's performance which is best left undone. . . . " Free Lance," in his writing, strongly advocates horses going without shoes of any kind, and tells us that the Arabs never shoe their horses, yet they perform long journeys without injury to the feet. He also tells us that he has seen thousands of unshod horses bringing cotton some three hundred miles up the country in South America over bad roads, and not one per cent. ever went lame or became foot-sore. " Free Lance " evidently is labouring under a mistake as regards the Arab and his horses, unless, indeed, they have much altered since the author was in their country ; they do not shoe their horse unless they are going long journeys, then they are not shod with iron, owing to the difficulty of obtaining that metal ; but they make a shoe of raw-hide which they nail to the feet ; this shoe will wear for a week or ten days, quite long enough to enable them to perform a long journey. The pack horses again in South America are certainly driven in droves to the Coast, with about one hundredweight of cotton on each horse, over roads bad enough for anything ; yet they have never been shod, and consequently they are as Nature formed them, and on the other hand they do not travel fast, and not compelled to go as men may guide them, but are perfectly at liberty to pick their way, and, sensible beasts that they are, will not put their feet upon anything likely to hurt them. Although horses may perform long journeys without shoes in America, South

Russia, and in Asia Minor, yet the author does not believe in unshod horses for general use in England ; not that our roads are worse, but we drive them much faster, consequently the horse has not a chance of picking his way, and therefore requires some protection to the crust of the foot. The tip being by far the best and safest of all the shoes that are made, Mr. Douglas found by careful experiment that light shoes will wear longer than heavy shoes. The contract farrier, by putting on heavy shoes, is wrong again, and, as I have said before, he begins his economy from the wrong end. I think 1 have said enough about the faults of shoeing, yet when I view the horse's foot with its beautiful structure and combinations, and see how it is cut, rasped, pegged to pieces with many and large nails, the heels cut open, sole and frog cut away, and last, but not least, heavy cumbersome lumps of iron put on for shoes, I cannot but come to the conclusion that although horses have been shod in England since the days of William the Conqueror, yet upon the whole our shoeing-smiths as a rule have not advanced in the art of shoeing, and many of our horses are shod now with as bad shoes as in the days of the Conqueror.

RANUNCULACÆ, OR BUTTERCUP POISONING.

June is the month in which fair flora puts forth all her charms, and although she clothes our fields and hedgerows with beauty of colour of every shade and form, yet her beauty may become fatal to man and beast if they do not understand the nature of the plants that are given them for food. Such is the instinct of the horse, that if left to roam in the field, and that field is overflowing with noxious herbs, he will refuse to eat them. Although the horse will eat hemlock with impunity, yet the common buttercups, *R. flammula, R. bulbus, R. sceleratus, R. acris,* and *R. arvensis,* are all of them injurious to the hungry horse, and many cases occur of serious illness which cannot be accounted for in any other way but from eating grass containing abundance of buttercup. It is a common practice with people who have one or two horses and a lawn for them to give their horses lawn-mowings to eat ; and as most lawns are mown by the machine, the sweet and good herbage becomes inseparably mixed with that of the *ranunculacœ,* and is given to the horse when it is hungry, when it will often eat it greedily, and in a short time alarming symptoms are set up. Buttercup poisoning is well known on the Continent, but happily it is not often met with in England, unless under exceptional circumstances. On the Continent it occurs by the horse eating the buttercup in the field, but in England it is never found unless the horse has had an abundance of cut grass given it when very hungry, after long journeys, or, as I have said, had lawn-mowings given it, especially if the season is dry, when the buttercup is much more acrid. The species of this plant popularly known as buttercup abounds everywhere in our pastures, and is so inextricably mingled with the herbage in some places as to make it appear doubtful whether it contains any acridity or causes the least annoyance to cattle, which must of necessity consume more or less of it while browsing in meadows where the plant is most abundant. Horses with their keen discriminating faculty uniformly avoid it, and hence its effects have rarely been observed unless it was given chopped up and mixed with corn. There are no less than fifteen species of ranunculus or crowfoot, natives of these islands, and common in our meadows and pastures, and most of them have more or less irritating properties ; those that are esteemed most irritating I have named above. The genus ranunculus is characteristic of a cold damp climate, poor wet soil, and is less acrid when grown in such situation than when grown in warm climates. It is asserted that an annual species, the *R. avensis*, has been proved to be fatal to sheep in Italy. Every part of the plant is pervaded by an acrid principle, which is volatile, and dissipated by heat or drying. The juice of the plant is a powerful vesicant, and prior to the introduction of cantharides, was used by medical men for that purpose. Owing, perhaps, to its universality and abundance in our pastures, it has become to be regarded as innocuous, or at least without suspicion of being productive of any bad effects. No cases, so far as I am aware, are recorded of its effects on cattle or sheep in this country, although its effects upon the latter have been observed on the Continent. Cases crop up from time to time in which horses are thought to be suffering from influenza, when, after a thorough investigation, the mischief is found in the horse having had lawn-mowings given it in which was an abundance of buttercup. The symptoms of poisoning by buttercup are first, a spasmodic action of the glottis, shortening and rigidity of the muscles of the neck, and violent contraction of the abdominal muscles, followed by a discharge of fluid through the nostrils; indeed, all the phenomena usually present in a complete act of vomition. In cases of vomiting, from rupture or overgorging with other kinds of food, the act is much more of a passive kind. There is a stretching out of the head and neck, little, if any, abdominal effort, and the peculiar spasmodic action in the pharyx is not observable until the return of the ingesta from the stomach, when a choking sound is heard during its passage through the posterior nares, when generally some of it falls back into the trachea, causing a fit of coughing, after which the head is extended, and the watery fluid trickles through the nostrils. I am inclined to believe that the action of the stomach is sufficient to effect this, and that a ruptured stomach is the result of vomiting, and not the cause of it. This, however, is a disputed point.

Mr. John Gerrard, M.R.C.V.S., of Market Deeping, gives us the following case, which I insert for the benefit of my readers. He says—" A five-year-old half-bred cob mare, the property of Sisson Martin, Esq., of Help-stoneheath, had been put to light work in the field from seven a.m. to three p.m. on the 15th of May; a quantity of lawn-mowings and hedge-side chippings were placed in the manger, of which she ate greedily, also a quarter in of oats and beans and some chaff; the usual quantity of water was given, and in about half-an-hour after she was placed in the stall she showed symptoms of abdominal pains, getting up and lying down and rolling violently. The usual colic drink was given, which temporarily relieved her. Two hours after she began to retch, and ,

as they thought, vomit; in consequence, I saw her at
eleven p.m., and no particular decided symptoms were
manifested; the pulse was 48 and soft, there was slight
tympanitis, the breathing was slightly accelerated, and
the temperature was normal. At intervals it was
seized with a peculiar spasmodic action of the throat,
as of difficulty of swallowing, and the eructations
occurring at intervals of fifteen minutes, and continuing
a few minutes, increasing in severity each time, until
the third occurrence, when a quantity—probably half-a-
pint of sour smelling fluid, mixed with portions of
badly masticated food was discharged through the
nostrils. This was followed by a fit of violent coughing, caused evidently by the passage of some fluid
into the larynx. I mentioned the probability of ruptured stomach to the owner; but from the absence of
any urgent symptoms always present in cases of rupture,
I thought it possible that the emesis might have
either been induced by the nature or more probably the
quantity of food consumed by the mare while in a
hungry and exhausted condition. I administered spirit
nitre æther two ounces, spirit ammonia aromat, one
ounce, ext. hyoscyomi one drachm, aq. menthæ. pip. two
ounces. This seemed slightly to allay the irritability of
the stomach, but the coughing and spasms continued for
some time, and about half-an-hour afterwards the mare
lay down. The spasms with occasional discharge of watery
fluid through the nostrils continuing, she lay quietiy on
her left side for an hour, when she got up, seemed easier,
and drank water. The pulse was 60 and full. I then
gave tinct. opii. two ounces in linseed gruel, and some oil-

cake gruel to drink. At four o'clock she seemed much better, so I gave a four-drachm physic ball and left. At eleven o'clock next day all the bad symptoms had disappeared. She would eat nothing, but drank small quantities of gruel, purging took place in twelve hours and continued for twenty-four, after which she gradually recovered. My attention was not directed to the character of the food until nineteen days afterwards, and when I visited the place where the grass had been cut from, it was a complete thicket of flowerless branches and roots of *ranunculacæ*, the characters of which I was unable to determine; from the absence of flowers and fruit, I was convinced that the food in question was largely composed of common buttercup, which the hungry, exhausted animal had greedily devoured. That the *ranunculacæ* possess acrid properties no one will deny, and that they are capable when taken in large quantity of inducing vomition in the horse may be fairly inferred. No other article of provender with which we are acquainted being capable of producing similar symptoms, even when the stomach is filled to repletion, and when rupture occurs through any other kind of food, there is never the same train of symptoms as are observed in all cases of *ranunculacæ* poisoning." The author has during the last few years met with many cases similar to the one above quoted, and has always adopted the same mode of treatment with the exception of administering one pint and a-half of linseed oil instead of a physic ball, and if there seems much irritation of the throat and coughing, stimulate the throat with white oils or Gregory's Versico Sudorific.

STOMACH STAGGERS.

This complaint, like the former, is often attributable to acrid substances taken into the stomach when the animal is in an exhausted state from long-continued labour. It is most frequently met with in the farm or cart horse, and is often the result of overfeeding, especially if the horse is fed upon food of bad quality. Farmers often resort to the false economy of selling all their good hay and corn, keeping only the worst for home consumption, and then are dreadfully disappointed when they find their stock in an unhealthy condition, and attribute the cause to everything but the right, viz,, their own foolish greed, grasping the shadow and losing the substance. Careless servants will too often neglect their horses, and afterwards, when food is placed before them while they are ravenously hungry, they swallow it rapidily and in too large a quantity without being properly masticated, consequently it swells in the stomach and stretches it far beyond its natural capacity; its action being thereby impaired, the brain is unduly acted upon, and giddiness and drowsiness induced, which occasion staggering. Too often the horse is kept short of water while abundance of food is placed before it, and instead of giving a little water before feeding and a small quantity of food at first to assist the animal in converting its food into a pulp and facilitating the operation of digestion, without a judicious quantity of water is given to the exhausted horse with its food, the stomach becomes gorged and the natural juices are inadequate to the performance of their office. It is no uncommon occurrence for farmers and others keeping a number of horses to lose several of them within very short periods of each other with this malady, from which an opinion prevails that this staggers is contagious. Nothing can be more erroneous than this belief, as it is quite certain it is the result of bad stable management or by overfeeding the horse with unwholesome food, or by the horse feeding too voraciously as already mentioned. This disease is much more common with old horses than young ones, owing to the want of vital energy in the digestive organs. Prevention in this complaint is again better than cure, and therefore I would strongly recommend owners of horses to look to them, and give some attention to the following :—Too much food given at one time after long fasting or hard work, or neglecting to give the animal water, is certain to produce staggers.

The hours of labour should be for limited spaces of time, with proper intervals of rest allowed, and the horse regularly fed during these intervals. Every man must have felt the effects of going without his dinner for three or four hours beyond the accustomed time. Exhaustion is sure to follow, which is produced by the juices acting upon the coating of an empty stomach. From five to six hours is the usual time between the meals of a labouring man, and with a horse that is worked no longer interval should elapse without feeding and watering. When persons are occasionally so situated that they cannot unyoke their horses at stated times for food and rest, they ought to carry hay and a nosebag with a supply of corn with them. Indeed, it is surprising, if they do not do it on the score of humanity, that they should be so blind to their own interests as to neglect having their horses watered and fed at proper intervals, and save the trouble, annoyance, and expense of having to call in the aid of the veterinary surgeon for a malady which by a trifling expense and a little judgment could be prevented. If nothing else is effective, self-interest ought to induce proper treatment. Staggers are said by some writers to often affect the horse when at grass. If the horse has previously been stinted with food, the author has never seen a well-defined case of staggers at grass and feels inclined to think that the so-called cases of staggers have been mistaken cases of *ranunculaceæ* poisoning, especially as he can find no case recorded of an animal dying of staggers at grass. Horses that have stomach staggers repeatedly are almost sure to go blind either partially or totally, from the effect of the gases engendered in the stomach acting on the nervous system and the optic nerve in particular. The symptoms of sleepy or stomach staggers is indicated by the dull, stupid, sleepy appearance of the horse, and the manner in which it staggers about in its stall. It seems unconscious of what it is doing, and if roused from its lethargy will probably take a mouthful of hay, and in a few seconds will desist from chewing it, the hay falling from its mouth. Many instances have occurred where the disease has been allowed to acquire such an ascendancy that the horse will drop down and die while in the act of eating. In other cases the drowsiness goes off, and is succeeded by delirium, and after falling, rising, and staggering about, will die in convulsions. The stomach staggers are indicated by a twitching of the muscles of the breast, and a yellowness of the eyes. Before a remedy is attempted, it must first be ascertained what has been the cause; the more so from the fact that mad staggers, in its early symptoms, are exactly the same. In this disorder it may be well supposed that medicine will have but little effect from the gorged state of the stomach. Some veterinary surgeons recommend bleeding, but for why it is impossible to tell, as no benefit is derived from it. That which debilitates the system can hardly be expected to assist the action of the stomach. Probably the best thing to do is to let nature work its own cure, by abstaining from giving food. As no certain cure is known, it is best to use prevention, and guard against it. The author has always adopted the following plan— Take away every particle of food, tie the horse's head up so that it cannot get at anything to eat, dissolve six drachms of Barbadoes aloes in warm water, and drench the horse with it; keep giving warm water at intervals, and when the stomach is relieved of its load, it may recover. Many instances occur of rupture of the stomach from expansion by confined gases. In every *post-mortem* I have made of subjects dying from stomach staggers, the stomach has been full of improperly masticated food; in some cases pieces of hay and straw were found in the stomach six inches long, that the hungry animal had swallowed without chewing.

MEGRIMS.

This is a malady occasioned by pressure on the brain caused by an unusual flow of blood to it. The flow of blood through the brain is quite ten times greater in quantity than through any other portion of the body of equal bulk. To prevent as far as possible any unusual flow of blood to this part, Nature has adopted a curious but, as usual, wise plan. The arteries are made to pursue an extremely winding and circuitous course, and enter the skull through small holes in the bony process. These holes are so small that they admit of but little enlargement of the blood-vessels, and thus to a great extent the chances of inflammation are lessened. Yet, notwithstanding this beautiful provision of an all-wise and far-seeing Creator, the horse is liable to be afflicted with disease of the brain, often from the want of brains in the so-called superior animal, man, by his subjecting the horse to violent and injudicious exercise and hard driving or riding in warm weather. It is but seldom that we find horses attacked with megrims when riding, and it seems principally horses in harness that are subject to this disease. Hard driving in warm weather forces the blood to the head, and distends the arteries of the head more than the veins, the consequence being that the small vessels covering the brain get gorged with blood, and then its bulk is increased to such an extent that it produces undue pressure upon the organs ot the nerves, which is followed by loss of power and even consciousness. Frequently the horse will stagger backwards and fall, the result being disastrous to the horse and all who may have the misfortune to be sitting behind it. A tight curb or collar with over-driving is too often the cause. It is a disease that is rarely met with except in the months of June, July, and August. Megrims is the name of the simplest form of inflammation arising from the above causes, and, as I have said before, it most commonly appears when the horse is over-driven. When attacked it will suddenly stop and shake its head, having been seized with giddiness and a slight degree of unconsciousness. If allowed to stop for a few minutes this will go off, and it will be enabled to proceed on its journey, but it not unfrequently happens that the attack is of a more severe kind, and under such circumstances will fall suddenly or run round two or three times and then fall. Sometimes it will lie quite quietly in a state of complete torpor, at other times it will struggle with great violence, yet still be unable to rise. In either of these conditions it will lie from five to ten minutes, when it will gradually resume sensibility, and then will be able to get upon its feet and proceed on its journey. After these attacks it generally exhibits symptoms of dullness and exhaustion. Immediately after the first attack of this disease resource should be had to bleeding, and that right plentifully. Three or four quarts of blood should be taken from the neck, which generally has the effect of arresting the symptoms. I am induced to the belief that in staggers there is an excess of fibrine in the blood, consequently copious bleeding will reduce the quantity of blood in the system at the time and allow nature to regain its equilibrium, and by the judicious administration of medicine enable the horse to make a fresh supply of pure blood. For this purpose give nitrate of potass three drachms every time the horse drinks ; give a physic ball composed of the following :—Barbadoes aloes six drachms, ginger two drachms, calomel two drachms, made with honey. When the horse is on a journey, and is attacked with this complaint, it is necessary to bleed from the bars (but this should not be resorted to unless the driver does not possess a lancet at the time the horse is attacked.) The bleeding-place in the palate is the third bar, in a direct line between the middle and second cutting teeth, and situated a little more than an inch within the mouth. Here the vein and artery make a curve, and a sharp penknife may be used and cut down upon the spot where they intersect each other, and the result will be a plentiful flow of blood, which will stop of its own accord when two or three quarts have issued forth. In consequence of the artery being cut across it will speedily shrink and cease to bleed, and the application of a piece of sponge or rag with cold water will stop the bleeding of the vein. In this operation the nerve is generally divided, but no evil effects will result from it. If the cut is made a little too much on one side, and nearly opposite the second incisor tooth, it is possible that the artery may be wounded longitudinally, but not divided, in which case there is great difficulty in stopping the flow of blood; the most effectual method of stopping which is to make a large pledget of lint or tow, as thick as a man's arm, roll it round a piece of string, put it across the horse's mouth, and tie the string across its nose. Then take a strap, and buckle it tightly round the horse's jaw, to prevent its opening its mouth and using its tongue to displace the pledget. This is sure to stop the bleeding. It is only when the horse is on a journey that the above mode of bleeding by cutting the bars should be resorted to, because there is no way to ascertain the quantity of blood taken, nor can the degree of inflammation be satisfactorily investigated, therefore it is only in cases of necessity that it is to be applied, as it may not only occasion much pain to the horse, but also a great deal of trouble to the operator.

The megrims is a very dangerous disease, not only to the horse, but to the driver, and in many instances the horse will die instantaneously, and frequently drop without the slightest previous indication of illness. If a horse has had one attack of this malady he is liable to a return of it, and is never to be trusted afterwards, although proper means have been adopted to prevent a recurrence of it. The most prudent plan is to part with the animal.

STAGGERS OR APOPLEXY.

This disease, like sleepy or stomach staggers, is caused by a deranged state of the digestive organs, and this in too many instances is the result of over-feeding and feeding with unwholesome food ; some persons are so foolish as to suppose that the horse may eat as much grain as it can consume, and that it will do no harm ; this is a serious mistake, for even without water the grain will swell in the stomach, and being over-loaded indigestion follows, the stomach being too much distended to allow it to perform its natural office, hence the head is affected. As in the animal economy a very intimate connexion exists between the brain and the stomach, each reciprocally influencing the other. The want of fresh air and exercise with horses that are over well-fed also tend strongly to derange the stomach, especially in warm weather. The bracing influence of exercise being wanted to give energy to the actions of the intestinal canal, the food frequently lodges there. This is also caused by the food being bad. Another cause is neglecting to water horses at regular intervals. This element is peculiarly necessary to animals living upon dry food. Every horse, as I have said before, should be watered regularly, cart horses at least four times each day, and in some cases when working very hard even more frequently in small quantities. In staggers of the apoplexy type, the symptoms are a low hanging of the head, either supporting it on the manger or extending it nearly to the ground; it moves to and fro while standing, and seems liable to fall at every movement. Its sight and hearing are much impaired, it will remain in this position from one to twelve hours, and then falls; its eyes are open and protruding, with a fixed seemedly unconscious stare, with the pupils much dilated; it grinds its teeth, the whole frame manifests twitchings, the vein of the neck is much inflected, its muzzle cold, and in attempting to swallow the drink is returned through the nostrils and mouth, and it dungs involuntarily; strong convulsive twitchings follow, and these are the certain prelude to death. In the first stage of this disease it comes on progressively with depression, sleepiness and feebleness, which is indicated by dulness of the eye, as it increases it presses its head against the wall or rack, and when aroused from this position it seems alarmed. In this complaint the remedies require to be prompt and severe, as any hesitation might prove fatal, therefore the veterinary surgeon should be called in at once, and while he is coming the vein of the neck should be opened, and as much blood taken as the animal will bear—from eight to ten quarts—according to the size of the horse.   After some time has elapsed this should be repeated, only a less quantity of blood taken, as in this complaint the animal makes blood fast.   If the lower intestines or rectum are overloaded with dung, the hand should be forced up the rectum, and the bowels relieved in this way.   If the animal exhibits symptoms of relief the following may be given in the form of a ball—Barbadoes aloes ten drachms, calomel two drachms, ginger three drachms, jalap half a drachm, mixed with honey to form a ball.   To many of my readers this will appear a large dose to give, but we must bear in mind that desperate diseases require desperate remedies, and unless the medicine in this case is sufficient to act at once on the nerves of the stomach, and thereby relieve the brain, our chances of success are small.   It is hardly necessary to remark again that this disease is in general very rapid, and the utmost prompti-tude must be exercised in the remedies.   In some instances the horse dies instantaneously whenever he falls, but whilst he lives there is hope of a cure, however severe the symptoms may appear, if we do not hesitate with our remedies.   In cases of this kind, where the symptoms are well defined, as I have stated above, the groom or farmers should act, for whilst they wait for the arrival of the veterinary surgeon, the horse may become past hope, and when the veterinary surgeon arrives he will find a dead horse. In these cases it is always advisable to give clysters which should be repeated every half-hour, until the bowels operate; the best and handiest clyster is composed of oatmeal gruel, three quarts, common salt three ounces, and olive oil half-a-pint. Some old writers recommend blowing cayenne up the nostrils, as well as powdered bark and spices, given internally, and blisters behind the ears; but these are perfectly useless, indeed, the former are perfectly ridiculous. Should the horse sufficiently recover to be able to take food, boiled barley, scalded bran, oatmeal, and lukewarm water may be given until he has recovered enough to eat hay, when the hay should be given in small quantities and of the best quality. After the horse has been subjected to the scouring-out principle, it is necessary to give medicine to give a tone again to the stomach, and set the digestive organs performing their offices; for this purpose the following will be given with advantage—lenetive electuary four ounces, cream of tartar four ounces, purified nitre two drachms, treacle two ounces, to be dissolved in hot ale, and given the first thing in the morning in a tepid state. This may be repeated two or three times, allowing two or three days to elapse between them. If the horse after this should not feed well, it may be necessary to give tonic medicine, and for this purpose obtain half a dozen tonic balls. I said in an early page of this work that I had placed a valuable receipt for tonic balls in the hands of Messrs. Perks and Llewellyn, chemists, Hitchin, which they will supply with full instructions, and they will be found all that are required to perfect a cure.

MAD STAGGERS OR BRAIN FEVER.

This disease is most frequently met with in the
heavy breeds of horses such as are used by millers,
brewers, and for farm purposes, and is caused by the
animals being too fat and too full of blood, by the chyle
having too strong a tendency to widen the vessels, and
especially so when the horse is overheated during warm
weather. The fever produced thereby causes a determination of blood to the brain, and thus terminating in
what is generally denominated brain fever. This disease proceeds from inflammation of the brain, and in its
earlier symptoms it cannot be distinguished from sleepy
or stomach staggers; it soon, however, assumes a
different character, the nostrils become distended, and it
commences to heave at the flanks, its eyes assume a
fixed vacant and wild stare, which is followed by complete delirium; it becomes furious and dashes about in a
violent manner from side to side, being quite unconscious
of its actions. The mad staggers are considerably alike
in their symptoms to rabies or common madness, and
also to colic. In the former of these maladies the horse
retains it consciousness, and the violence of its actions
will depend upon the peculiar character of its madness.
In some instances a desire to be mischievous is manifested; in colic the horse rises and falls, although not in
a violent manner. Sometimes, however, it plunges, but
in most cases it rolls itself about, and frequently looks
towards its flanks with an evident expression of suffering
from pain. The treatment of this disease is at all times

extremely uncertain, profuse bleeding is strongly recommended by most writers; open the jugular vein on both sides and take as much blood as will cause the horse to fall, or if it is down at the time, until it manifests evident signs of exhaustion; after this give newly-powdered croton nut half a drachm, or croton oil 20 drops. Upon no occasion give more than half a drachm of the nut or 20 drops of the oil, as cases are not wanting where 30 drops of croton oil have killed heavy powerful horses, which were previously in good health. The croton should be given in a drink of oatmeal and water every six hours, after which ten grains of nut or five minims of oil may be given until the bowels are freely moved; to assist in which, injections of warm soap and water should be often used. In using croton nut or oil, from its acrid properties, we make the horse's throat and mouth very sore, therefore it should never be used unless in a case of extreme necessity. I have no doubt but the following would have quite as beneficial an effect without the irritating effects:—One ounce of aloes dissolved in a pint of water, afterwards two drachms every four hours until it operates, after this such medicine should be given as has a tendency to diminish the quantity of blood sent out from the heart. Foxglove in drink doses of one drachm each every six or eight hours, or tartar emetic can be given alternately with the foxglove in one drachm doses.

If the above treatment does not arrest immediately the disease, death is sure speedily to follow. Sometimes cases occur with horses at grass which are mistaken for mad staggers, but, although producing alarming symptoms, is of an entirely different nature, being no other than poisoning by the bearded darnel (*Lolium temulantum*).   Doubtless much mischief is caused by this grass to horses, sheep, and cattle—firstly, by an improper quantity after long confinement to other food ; and secondly, by the irritation caused by the rough bristles or styles with which these are armed.   The darnel grass, however, possesses also narcotic as well as irritant properties, the seeds especially being prolific in their soporific powers.   This species of darnel grows wild in many parts of England in fields among wheat and barley, and flowers early in July ; it varies greatly in appearance so as sometimes to be confounded with rye grass, *Lolium perenne,* which is a useful and wholesome fodder. Many undoubted cases of injurious consequences following from eating bread in which the seed of the darnel has been ground up with corn are on record.   It is stated in the *Medical and Surgical Journal* that about eighty persons in the poor-house at Sheffield, after breakfasting on oatmeal porridge, in which it appears that the seeds of the darnel had been ground, were seized with the usual symptoms of poisoning ; violent agitation of the limbs, convulsive twitchings, confusion of sight, and extreme pains in the forehead, were observed in nearly all those persons.   It seems they were relieved with copious draughts of vinegar and ultimately recovered.   When a person is supposed to be poisoned by eating darnel the best thing to do is to give an emetic, and afterwards partake freely of acidulated drinks.   The signs of poisioning by darnel in the horse are abdominal irritation with occasional diarrhœa, tenesmus, tucked-up appearance of the flanks, anorexia, nausea, irregular respiration, slow and soft pulse, decline of animal heat, vertigo, staggering gait with crossing of the legs, amaurosis, listlessness, coma, and death. These signs are sometimes mistaken again in their turn for acute indigestion and nervous apoplexy. When the horse has eaten darnel and produced the effects of poisoning there is no antidote known to counteract its effect that we can use with reliance ; for empty its stomach we cannot with an emetic, therefore reliance must be placed upon powerful catharties, stimulants, and the treatment of apoplexy and narcotic poisoning generally. The first thing to do is to empty its stomach, which must be done by the slow process of purging, and nothing is better than one pint and a-half of linseed oil, given milk warm. After that has purged give a four-drachm aloes ball, then tonic medicine to restore the appetite. The difference between darnel poisoning and nervous apoplexy is known by the absence of all cerebral disturbance, weak pulse which is sometimes small but not usually rapid ; the appetite remains, there is also a general vivacity, but the bowels are usually constipated and there is little fever present. The limbs do not always lose their powers of movement although the ability to stand is absent. These cases are best treated by the practical veterinary surgeon, as it is necessary to use *nox vomica* in minute doses, and also strychnine, which being very dangerous drugs should only be used by practical men.

There is yet another disease with which the horses is at times affected, which is sometimes mistaken for mad staggers. The cases are rare ; happily it is so. This disease is

RABIES OR MADNESS.

The symptoms of which are that while the horse is apparently in good health it will stop all of a sudden, be seized with a trembling all over its body, will paw the ground violently, heave heavily, stagger, and fall down ; in a few seconds it will rise again and proceed a little way on its journey, when it will again stand still, look anxiously about and will again come down, it will again get up and is then seized with a paroxysm of frenzy, attempting to bite everything that comes in its way, and will kick and plunge in a most fearful manner, and if in a stable will strike the wall or the sides of its stall, or indeed any object that may be near, until the perspiration stands upon its whole body like foam.   The animal is seized with almost insatiable thirst, and will remain in a quiescent condition for some hours, when another paroxysm will ensue; these fits will succeed each other at intervals for two or three days, when a termination will be put to them by death.   It is neither safe nor wise to keep the horse alive under such circumstances.   If the owner is uncertain if it is rabies, the animal should be slung; this will prevent it injuring itself or others who have the charge of it.   The symptoms, however, are well marked, and the sooner the animal is dead and buried the better, as there is no chance of its recovery. When symptoms of rabies have manifested themselves it is in vain to attempt a cure, but in cases where horses have been bitten by dogs, whether they appear harmless at the time or not, they should have the wound deeply burned out with lunar caustic. This incurable complaint is caused by the bite of a rabid animal of some kind, generally a dog. Horses have been known to be seized with rabies simply from having licked a mad dog after death. The writer once saw a mad horse in Knightsbridge Barracks, which broke both jaws in biting the manger, and when found the next morning was trying to seize the manger with the broken stumps of the jaw, all its top teeth being knocked out and its bottom jaw broken off just below the tusk. The animal was of course instantly shot.

TETANUS OR LOCK-JAW.

This disease to human beings as well as to the horse generally proves fatal, yet as the writer has been successful in two cases, the mode of treatment adopted will not be out of place in these pages. This disease does not manifest itself of a sudden, but generally steals over the system by slow and insidious means. It first develops itself by the animal appearing heavy, dull, and unwell for a day or two. It feeds sparingly, frequently half chewing its food, then letting it drop from its mouth. When it drinks, the water is gulped instead of the ordinary mode of taking it. The action of the jaw becomes extremely imperfect, and the saliva trickles from the sides of its mouth. The mouth at length can be but imperfectly opened, and ultimately the whole of the voluntary muscles of the neck and upper portions of the shoulders become immovably fixed. After this there is

no hope of the mouth being opened again, and the
horse, if not killed, must die of starvation, in a short
time nearly all the muscles of the body becoming spas-
modically affected. The cause of this disease proceeds
from the nerves being injured in consequence of a
wound having been received by one of the ligaments or
tendons.   It sometimes comes on by an injury to
the foot from the puncture of a nail; nicking and dock-
ing are often the cause of it.   One case that I had was
caused by the waggoner cracking his whip in front of
the horse's head, the point of the lash striking the
horse on the ball of the eye, hurting the optic nerve.
It sometimes comes on instantaneously after the in-
fliction of the wound, and sometimes not until a considerable time after.   It is caused sometimes by the
animal being allowed to cool too suddenly when very
warm; worms have also been known to be the remote
cause of tetanus; bots have also produced it.

The usual way in which this disease comes on
seldom leads to no suspicion of what it is, as few who
have not previously watched its progress can trace its
character.   Hence it has assumed its climax before
persons are aware of it.   In this condition it can seldom
be cured, from the difficulty of administering medicine.
In this affection the endermic method of administering
remedies bids fair to become beneficial; prussic acid,
morphia, atropine, conium, &c., or tinctures of plants
containing the last three substances are readily brought
to bear upon the system by the endermic syringe.
Injections also per anum of chloric ether and its allies
prove serviceable, and in the trassmatic form the

benumbing effects of carbolic acid, as used in the antiseptic treatment, are frequently of great service in reducing the intensity of the paroxysms. It is not prudent to rely upon the one uninterrupted exhibition of one agent beneath the skin; they should be alternated with each other, and used occasionally as mixtures, where no risk of chemical union and destruction is feared. That neglected branch of veterinary therapeutics —galvanism, should be tried, as much benefit is derived ofttimes from it, opposite poles of the instrument being placed at the extremities of the spine, and maintained there with wet sponges or cloths for some hours; where these measures are insisted upon, that former *sine qua non*—catharsis, is dispensed with.

The symptoms in the first case that came under my care were very intense, and the temperature ascended to 103 degrees and ultimately to 104 degrees. The treatment consisted in administering muriate of morphia, introduced by injections into two subcutaneous pouches, formed by a seton-needle in the masseteric region, or what most of my readers would call its cheek. The seton-needle was passed under the skin from above in an oblique form, from about three inches under the eye; these subcutaneous pouches were about four inches deep, one on each cheek. The quantity of the alkaloid injected each day at various times was one gramme in 50 grammes of distilled water; a liniment composed of turpentine and liquid ammonia was rubbed into the skin across the loins, and enemas of soap and water, each containing twelve grammes of laudanum, were frequently given. Hot fomentations were constantly applied day and night, for which purpose two thick horsecloths were constantly placed in boiling water, wrung out and put on the horse as hot as possible. Chloroform and sulphuric either were also prescribed; these were placed on a piece of sponge and held under the nostrils for the horse to inhale its fumes. The animal was placed in a stable and kept moderately warm. This treatment was continued night and day for three days, at the termination of which the animal was better. The muscular tension had diminished, the respiration was perceptibly better, and the jaws could be opened to the breadth of two fingers. With this amelioration in the symptoms the animal gave evidence of relief by frequently drinking oatmeal gruel, in which were large doses of tartar emetic and nitrate of potash. This treatment was persevered with for ten more days, and gradually brought about an amendment.

On the twenty-fourth day from the receipt of the injury, and the thirteenth of medical treatment, the medicines hitherto administered were discontinued, and eight grammes of bromide of potassium was given daily with enemas now and then, and dry frictions were substituted until the thirtieth day. At this time the animal began to eat slowly of bran mash, and afterwards damp forage, but it was not until above two months from the commencement of convalescence that it had perfectly recovered. The old fashioned-method of bleeding for tetanus has almost died out, and many cases are now on record in which the beneficial effects of hydrate of chloral have been proved, in many instances no other agent being used, enemas and hot fomentation excepted. Dr. Coryllos gives us two cases which he cured with chloral; he administered from one drachm and a-half to two drachms each day. In one case he gave in all three ounces and a-half in twenty days, in another of longer duration he gave six ounces of chloral hydrate, and both cases recovered. M. Verneuil gives two cases in the *Societé de Chirurgie de Paris*, when he gave a drachm and a-half of chloral in twenty-four hours, and in another case he gave two drachms and a-half in twenty-four hours. He recommends beginning by administering chloral by the mouth instead of intraneous injections. He cured five successive cases of tetanus with chloral hydrate.

These cases are sufficient to show that with care, patience, and perseverance, tetanus may be overcome; but without the groom is a good nurse. the veterinary surgeon stands a poor chance of having many successful cases of tetanus. It is mainly to the effects of nursing, combined with a rational administering of medicine, that tetanus can be cured. In administering medicine it is necessary to use considerable caution, as the rigidity of the muscles of the neck occasion much pain to the horse if the head be elevated. It is always best to give medicine in a liquid form and through a tube; most practical veterinary surgeons keep a tube made for the purpose. In tetanus the digestive functions are not impaired, and the poor animal suffers much from hunger, and to keep up the system as much as possible, thick gruel should be given by the aid of a tube.

GLANDERS.

Of all the diseases that are incidental to the horse, there is none to compare to this most malignant and most to be dreaded in a steed. The instant there is any appearance of it the horse should be removed to a place by itself, as this malady is extremely infectious, and from want of due caution whenever a suspicion of it is entertained, the most disastrous consequences may result. Although glanders has been known to mankind for upwards of 1800 years and the symptoms well described, yet it is lamentable to state that up to the present hour no cure has been found for it. No disease to which the horse is subject has had more experiments made with it, and all have proved equally unsatisfactory, and although many cases are reported of horses having been cured of glanders, yet when the same treatment adopted has been applied to an undoubted case of glanders it has always turned out a disappointment. Many men have also lost their lives by becoming inocculated with the fœtid pus from the nostril, and fearful indeed is the death of a man from this loathsome disease. Medical remedies have alleviated the severity of this disease for a time and arrested its progress, but it is certain to return and prove fatal at last, and it is doubtful if ever a case of *true* glanders was ever cured. There are various diseases which in their early stages have much the same appearance as glanders, and therefore it is necessary to watch them narrowly, as of course perfect recovery may follow. The very first symptoms of glanders is a constant discharge from the left nostril of mucus, clearer and of a lighter colour than in common cold or catarrh, and more glutinous in its substance. If rubbed between the finger and thumb it has a sticky feel. This discharge also differs from common cold by being continuous, whereas in the latter it is only discharged at intervals. The matter discharged in this disease differs from that of a common catarrh in its specific gravity. If a small quantity is dropped into water it sinks, and it will not mix with water if stirred with it; whereas the mucous discharge of a common cold swims near the surface, and preserves its slimy consistence although stirred, and will not comingle with it.

A singular character of the glanders is that it always attacks the left nostril, very few cases having ever been seen in which the horse was glandered in the right nostril. Mr. Dupay, a celebrated veterinary surgeon and director of the School of Surgery at Toulouse, mentions that out of eight hundred cases of glanders which came under his care during his practice, only one was affected in the right nostril. Shortly after the discharge from the nostril takes place, the horse becomes affected in the glands of the lower jaw, which swell to a considerable extent, and ultimately become attached to the bone. Another character by which this disease is well known is, that at no time is the discharge from the nostrils accompanied by a cough. Some considerable time after the discharge has made its appearance, the gluey substances will be seen accompanying the mucous discharge. It is this pus, mingling with the other gluey matter, which, absorbed by the circulating vessels and carried to the gland, affects it. However, in common cold the gland is sometimes swelled, but in the real glanders the swelling generally subsides considerably in a short time, and the glands are not in the centre of the channel, but firmly adhere to the jaw. This is a never failing test of the disease, and besides, it is quite certain that if the discharge flows from both nostrils it is not glanders. At this stage of the disease the mucous membrane of the nostril becomes dark purple or of a livid colour, sometimes of a tone intermediate between the two shades. In some instances there is inflammation of those parts which varies from the common appearance, being of a purple cast instead of the high red which usually accompanies inflammation. This is followed by the formation of small circular tubercles on the lining of the nostrils, and these in a short time ulcerate and discharge puss. When this has taken place, there can no longer be a doubt that the horse is glandered, and care must be taken not to mistake the lacrymal or tear-duct for an ulcer. This duct is a continuation of the skin of the muzzle, which is situated a little way up the nostril, while the ulcerated tubercles are placed upon the mucus membrane above the duct, and well marked by a line of separation. After the formation of tubercles, the animal is sure to have become constitutionally affected, its coat will stare and fall off, it will lose flesh, and its belly will be tucked up. Cough will follow, the appetite will be much affected, accompanied by a rapid diminution of strength, the tubercles will multiply, discharge will be more abundant, and will assume a purulent and bloody appearance, accompanied by a very fœtid smell. The ulceration will extend down to the windpipe, and the lungs will be in a very short time studded with tubercles, a test that the lungs have become affected; the breathing will be difficult, and a stifled grating noise accompanies it, which is a certain prelude to death. A common catarrah has often been mistaken for glanders, but a little attention will soon enable any one to perceive the distinction between the two diseases. Catarrh is usually accompanied with fever, sore throat, general cough, loss of appetite, and a discharge from both nostrils, and in most cases very copious, sometimes purulent; the glands are generally swollen on both sides of the throat, and are moveable and hot to the touch. The proper means being adopted all the symptoms are abated.

Strangles have also been mistaken for glanders, and usually affects young horses only. At first they resemble a comon cold with a severe cough and wheezing, accompanied with considerable thickening and swelling between the jawbones, the swelling becoming harder towards the middle, a fluid can be felt in the centre, which ultimately breaks, and a discharge flows from it. The mucous-membrane of the nostrils is of a very red colour, and an ample discharge continues which is mixed with pus from nearly the commencement. The remote cause of glanders has hitherto baffled all the members of the veterinary art, its true history being still unknown, and the unsatisfactory theories of medical authors throwing no light on it. All that can be gained by the perusal of numerous works upon this disease by past and present authors is that the disease is highly contagious. All authors agree as to the symptoms, and but little differ-

K

ence is expressed as to the cause. That it is equally fatal to man is proved by the deaths that take place from time to time of men having become inocculated with the disease through some accidental cause. The *South Durham Herald,* of March 28th, 1874, alludes to the sad fact that a miner at the Castle Eden Colliery had died from blood poisoning consequent upon the introduction of the virus of glanders into his system. The extract I make relating to this melancholy occurrence says " That Joseph Hall, a miner, washed his hands in a trough from which a pony suffering from this disease had drunk, he at the time having an open wound on his right hand. The day following his hand was much swollen, the swelling gradually increased, and in a short time his whole body was a mass of corruption. He died on Wednesday morning. Dr. Wilson, who had attended him, gave a certificate that the deceased died from blood poisoning, caused by inocculation from a glandered horse. The deceased was only 24 years of age, and had been recently married." In the same month we find this note made in the *Veterinary Record,* " A veterinary surgeon of the French Army, named M. Nicoulean, had died from acute glanders, the result of inocculatian while dissecting the carcase of a horse which was affected with that disease. The submaxilliary lymphatic of the animal was enlarged, and the characteristic discharge and ulceration were present, but the unfortunate gentleman could not trace any signs of the distinctive tubercles in the pulmonary tissue notwithstanding the most careful search, and in cutting the mucous membrane of the nostril his knife slipped and punctured his finger. Notwithstanding that every precaution was taken and everything done for him that medical science could suggest, he died in a few days after suffering untold agony." Numerous other cases can be quoted of men dying of this malignant disease, but the two cases above are enough to show how necessary it is to proceed with the utmost caution, if it is only expected that a horse is inflicted with glanders. The remote cause of glanders is we fear to be found in ill-ventilated and badly drained stables; there the ammonia from the urine fills the whole atmosphere, which being constantly inhaled ultimately produces a poisonous effect upon the lungs, caused by an undue quantity of oxygen being inhaled; besides the constant irritation which it must naturally produce upon that delicate portion of the mucous membrane, which is the organ of smell, it induces the formation of those tubercles which once formed can never be eradicated. We find that glanders almost always breaks out in ill-ventilated stables, and which are likewise kept too hot. Fracture of the nasal bone has been said to produce it in some few instances, as well as a long continued and inveterate catarrah with a constant and irritating discharge from the nostrils. We find that in the lofty well-aired stables of gentlemen this disease is comparatively little known, and when it does show itself in such it has in all probability been introduced by some fresh importation to the stud of one or more horses previously affected. In such a case all the animals in the stable may catch the malady, as glanders is well known to be highly contagious. In many of the crowded and ill-aired stables of London and other large towns this disease is but too often an inmate, and frequently great havoc is wrought among the horses in consequence. Many horses become affected with glanders by being put into a stall in which a glandered horse has been standing; this is often the case in a livery stable. The glandered horse is bought at a fair or market and brought to a livery stable to be fed, the pus from its nostrils drops into the manger and the next horse that is fed out of the same manger becomes innoculated with the pus; especially if it happens to have a slight scratch upon his muzzle, and it comes in contact with the crib on which the mucous of the glandered animal has been left, and is thus carried into the circulation of the blood. All stalls, and especially public stables, should have high divisions between them to prevent the muzzles of horses coming in contact with each other. Horses being very apt to smell each other indeed it is by this faculty alone they recognise each other and distinguish their companions. From an ill-judged piece of economy many persons, after being aware that one of their horses is glandered, persist in keeping it in the same stable with others and by so doing is every hour risking all they possess. It is the duty of every person as soon as he is certain of his horse having caught this disease to destroy it as speedily as possible, for although a glandered horse may be able to work for a considerable time under the influence of this disorder, he wlll find ultimately that it is a bad piece of economy to keep it. Many persons who have lost horses by this disease have resorted to extremes to prevent a continuance of it. Some have gone so far as to pull down the stable, and others have taken out all the internal fittings, putting one in mind of the "Industrious Irishman," who pulled the stairs down to keep the bugs out of the bedroom. It is quite sufficient if the mangers and other parts which the nostril of the glandered horse has touched, be thoroughly scrubbed with hot water and strong soda, and afterwards with chloride of lime ; the proportion of which should be one pint and a half to a pailful of water ; or carbolic acid and hot water, which should be in proportion of half-a-pint to two gallons of water. The walls should be limewashed, and all the cloths, headstalls, and halters destroyed, and the iron-work painted. We have already said that we cannot find a well-authenticated case of cure of the glanders. Hinde says : "Glanders has been cured spontaneously on a large scale, under his own inspection solely by regular and good living, a fine seaside country and moderate work being the only adjuncts, with such an auxiliary as Venice turpentine diffused in steam up the nostrils have removed recent cases of glanders, wherein the skankers were already visible, the discharge fœtid, and the glander hard and fixed. To apply this remedy make a bran mash hot in which is mixed the turpentine, attach this to the horse's head by means of a nose bag, and in a quarter of an hour renew the heat by means of a pailful of hot water in which the bag is to be partially immersed, afterwards cover the body, head, and neck, so as to promote perspiration ; but if it does not come on by these means, cover the body first in a blanket that has been immersed in hot water and wrung out, rub dry, cover up, and repeat the same daily. In all such cases we have given salt in every way the patient could take it in its food and water, and wash its nose and legs with salt and water. With the same view we hear of sulphate of iron being given in the water, the pail being suspended in the stable for the animal to drink at pleasure. I have given the above upon the authority of Mr Hinde, but we have known it tried without effect. Whether this loathsome and fatal disease has its origin in the deteriorated atmosphere of stables is a problem that has not yet been solved, there is little doubt, however, that a strong preventitive is found in a clean, cool, well-aired stable, and exposing the horse as much as possible to the influence of the atmosphere. The glanders is unknown among the Arabian horses, in South America, and in Circassia, where horses are not confined in stables. As a word of caution to all my readers who may have to buy horses at fairs from dealers of whom they know nothing, it is necessary they should have their eyes open because by infamous trickery they too frequently use means to deceive the purchaser. It is a well-known fact that if a glandered horse is galloped hard the increased action of the lungs in breathing will thoroughly drive the mucous substance out of the nostrils, and to make it continue dry for a time they blow up the diseased nostril (the left) powdered allum, or white vitrol, but a little attention will enable anyone to see that the animal is in pain and will make ineffectual attempts to sneeze. The foetid smell, so different from any other discharge, will convince even the inexperienced person that the horse is glandered.

A favourite trick of the horse dealer is to gallop the

blow vitrol up its nostril, and then force a pledget of cotton wool a considerable way up its nostril, they will try to destroy the fœtid smell by syringing a solution of carbolic acid up the right nostril.   In buying a horse at a fair always lay hold of its nostril and pinch both together so as to stop the horse's breath, hold it so for a few seconds, then let go your hold and the horse will blow its nose violently; if it has been " plugged " the horse will blow the pledget out, and if it does so it is glandered without a doubt.

FARCY.

This disease is nearly allied to glanders ; some have supposed it to be a modification of that malady. This, however, is a great mistake, they are essentially different, as I will endeavour to point out.   It is the decided opinion of every eminent veterinary surgeon that glanders is incurable ; farcy, however, is not so.   The first symptoms manifested of farcy are the appearance of small tumours, popularly called farcy buds or buttons, situate close to some of the veins, and following their courses, being connected together with a kind of cord— hence they are called corded veins by farriers and veterinary surgeons.   At first they are generally small, and consequently may not be noticed for some weeks, until they have attained their full size, after which they usually increase more rapidly, become hot, and cause considerable pain, and at length ulceration ensues. They first make their appearance about the face, neck, and throat, sometimes extending to the inside of the thigh, and produce lameness and considerable swelling of the limb. A fœtid discharge generally proceeds from both nostrils (in glanders only one, and that the left), which, in the process of time assumes all the malignant characters of glanders, and is equally contagious. It sometimes happens that farcy is progressing in the constitution long before the buds make an appearance or swelling along the course of the absorbent take place ; in some instances the buds are not ulcerated, but assume a callous texture, in which case they are very difficult to reduce. At this period a check of the disease takes place, and many persons are led to believe that the disease is cured, as the horse seems to have quite recovered. This, however, is only a delusion, and though no symptoms of the complaint manifests itself for months, it is working in secret, and its malignant effects are sure to show themselves sooner or later, and all at once break out in a most malignant form, and in all probability in a few days death will close the scene. Sometimes a considerable swelling takes place about the head, especially in the region of the muzzle, and from which an extremely fœtid mucous fluid is discharged, various portions of the body will assume a mangy appearance, swelling in the limbs will follow, the heels will become cracked, and exhibit all the appearance of grease, the animal in most cases becoming emaciated and weak. Farcy assumes many different appearances in its various stages. It is no uncommon thing for one hind leg to swell suddenly to a large size, accompanied by abrupt projections and depressions, and which the poor animal will be unable to move. This is generally accompanied with a considerable degree of fever. The above swelling differs considerably from that which is usually called farcy humour; in this the skin presents a red and shining appearance, from the whole surface of which exudes a thin fluid, accompanied by great lameness, the fetlock is round, tumid, and smooth, and swollen as far as the heel. This disease is in consequence of being over fed, and the want of proper exercise at the same time. Painful and disagreeable as this malady is, frequent fomentations of a decoction of marsh-mallows, and smart doses of medicine will speedily reduce the swelling, and especially if the swollen part is well rubbed and the horse subjected to exercise. There is no doubt that the cause of farcy is to be looked for in bad stable management, want of exercise, and infection. There have been many cases in which it could not be accounted for upon any other principle than that it was contagious. In certain localities it has been known to be prevalent where horses could not have come in contact with one another, yet, strange as it may appear, we have it upon good authority, that horses in the field have taken glanders from affected animals which were in the fields half-a-mile away. A few years ago a number of horses became affected with glanders in a field which had a swift running brook passing though it. After a thorough investigation it was found that a badly-glandered horse was turned out in a field half-a-mile up the stream, and no doubt the pus from its nostrils falling into the stream was carried down by the current, and the horses lower down became innoculated with it, thus spreading this foul disease in all directions. In the early stages of farcy, the horse should be subjected to gentle doses of medicine. The following is often given for this disease:—Barbadoes aloes eight drachms, Castile soap two drachms, liquorice powder half an ounce, made into a ball. Others recommend the following in its stages:— Corrosive sublimate half a drachm, powdered aniseed one ounce, mixed with syrup into three balls; these to be continued for ten days in succession. These balls containing a preparation of mercury (corrosive sublimate), it is necessary to keep the animal warm while this medicine is being given. With some constitutions it does not agree, and in such cases I have found half a drachm of opium given in a ball have good effect, but should it not prove effectual, the same quantity may be given twelve hours afterwards, that is if purging and staleing is produced in too strong a degree. The above quantity is a dose for a horse of a delicate constitution, and should always be given first. If the horse is of a more robust habit, the dose may be increased after a few days to double the quantity.

The above applies to the stage of this disease when the farcy buds are unbroken; if any of them have begun to ulcerate the welding iron should be brought to a dull red heat and gently applied to them, but if upon feeling you find they are filled with matter even although they have not broken, they should have an application of the iron. This should be carefully examined for some days afterwards, and if they exhibit an unhealthy spongy appearance, and a thin gluey matter issues from them, they should be frequently washed with corrosive sublimate two drachms, spirit of wine four ounces, or, what I have proved equally as good, carbolic acid one ounce, boiling water one quart, well agitated; this should be continued until the bottom of the ulcers assume a healthy colour, of a clear red appearance, and the spongy foul look has disappeared. When this is the case the matter discharged will have completely changed its aspect, and instead of being thin and glary, it will have become thick, and of a white or yellowish colour. At this stage some writers recommend an application of Friar's balsam, but I have quite discarded that, as I find a much better substitute in carbolised oil. During this treatment other buttons may be found to contain matter, and these should be subjected to the same treatment. This is a nasty disease, and requires great attention and a long course of treatment to insure a cure. At this stage the disease will have attacked the constitution, it will therefore be necessary for a more rigid medical treatment, and it may be found necessary to give an alterative composed of corrosive sublimate ten grains, gentian two drachms, ginger one drachm; to be given morning and evening until the ulcers have dried up. Sometimes this acts violently as a purgative, at other times the horse's mouth becomes sore, in which case one drachm of sulphate of copper should be substituted for the corossive sublimate. It not unfrequently happens in this disease that one kind of medicine when administered loses its effect, and it may be necessary to give medicine alternately or a combination of medicines, such as the following:—Sulphate of copper three drachms, corrosive sublimate one scruple, powdered bark two drachms, powdered ginger two drachms, mixed with Venice turpentine, to form three balls, and give morning and evening.

Probably in a few days the above may have to be given in two balls to produce the desired evacuations, but should the intestines be moved too freely, recourse must be had to the opium ball as given above. During this treatment the horse should be kept apart from the other, and the stable disinfected with carbolic acid, and its food should consist of green provender, carrots, turnips, mangolds, mash or any other soft food, but corn should upon no account be given except in moderate quantities. It should be freely exposed to the air, and if in the summer season it should be turned out in the field for four or five hours daily; it should be carefully stabled during the night, as its system, with the above course of treatment, will be open, and will be very liable to take cold. In the winter, when the weather is fine, it should be walked out for an hour or two in the middle of the day regularly.

Some people prefer the following instead of the firing iron, but its effects are not so certain. Muriatic acid two drachms, muriate of mercury one drachm, to be well mixed, then add pure water four drachms, spirit of wine six drachms. Should this be found to cause too much irritation more water must be added. In applying the above it should be done with a small piece of sponge tied on the end of a piece of stick; as it is a powerful caustic and will blacken the hands of the operator; if touched with it should be washed off immediately, as the skin will continue black until it is worn away. In cases which severe salivation ensues from the use of corrosive sublimate (which

is in fact a preparation of mercury) which not unfrequently happens with horses of delicate constitution,
the following purgative should be given :—Rochelle
salts seven ounces, sulphur two and a-quarter ounces,
mixed with liquorice powder and treacle, and formed
into a ball, to be repeated for two or three days.
If the limbs are much swollen the carbonate of potass
may be given every time the animal drinks. Warm
fomentations should be constantly applied to the limbs
with cloths, as hot as the animal can bear it, or flannel
bandages, put on and kept constantly wet with hot water,
as hot as a man can bear his hand in it. After all
treatment, even the most successful kind, I doubt if it
is entirely got out of the system, as all animals, having
once had farcy, are liable to a return of it at any time.

NASAL GLEET.

This is another disease that has sometimes been
mistaken for glanders, but it is quite distinct from it in
its affecting both nostrils, and also being a discharge of
clear pus. There is a constant discharge of a thickish
fluid from the nostrils, proceeding from the mucous
membrane which lines the nostrils in the internal
cavity. This disease is frequently brought on by the
effects of a long-continued discharge from catarrh or
cold. It is unattended with any feverish symptoms;
the flow of this thick mucous gleet is often very considerable and variable in colour. When the horse is
living upon green food it often assumes a greenish hue,
and sometimes even a grass-green colour. If its diet is
of dry food, and it is kept in the stable, then it assumes

a very different hue, varying from cream-white to brown
or straw colour, and mixed with pus ; in some instances
this is mixed with blood. This discharge is sometimes
continuous, and at others it is only occasionally squeezed
out : in the latter case it is generally thick, and when so
the disease is generally on the wane.   If, however, it is
of long duration, it sometimes assumes a serious aspect,
and may ultimately prove fatal.   Sometimes this
disease is accompanied with cough, and when it is so,
the writer has found very good results from the
following pectoral balls, given every day for a week.
They are also very good for horses suffering from
asthma or chronic cough :—Balsam of capivi, Barbadoes tar and Castile soap, of each four ounces, prepared
kali one ounce, beat them together in a mortar, then
add carraway seed, aniseed, grains of paradise, and
liquorice powder, of each four ounces, sufficient honey
or treacle to form it into a stiff paste.   Give two ounces
each day for three days, then every other day for a
week, and afterwards one or two a week.   The writer
frequently stimulates the nostrils with the fume of
vinegar, and for this purpose make a brick red hot, and
put a horse cloth over the horse's head, holding the
brick on a shovel under the cloth, and pouring gently
the vinegar on to the brick.   The fumes are confined
in the rug, and the animal is forced to inhale it.   This
will be found to cleanse the nostrils and heal the
irritation of the mucous membrane.   If the disease is
of long standing it may be as well to use Venice
turpentine alternately with the vinegar.   For this
purpose the turpentine should be mixed with bran,

and put into a nose-bag, boiling water poured upon it, and then put upon the horse's head; when it begins to get cool the bag should be immersed again in hot water to keep up the steam. In slight cases the following may be found to be all that is necessary to effect a cure:—One ounce of sulphate of copper made into a ball with linseed meal and treacle, twice a day. This disease, although discharging a quantity of mucous and pus, is neither infectious nor contagious, although if left unattended to it may assume in a secondary stage a serious aspect.

STRANGLES.

This disease is incidental to all horses in their youth, and indeed looked upon as a baby's complaint. It attacks the colt generally between the age of two and three years, though sometimes the colt may escape until it is four or even five years old; in some few cases old horses will have it, when it is very difficult to cure. High-fed colts generally have it sooner than those which are fed upon a lower diet. Neither the remote nor the approximate cause of this complaint is known. It appears to be in some degree analogous to the small-pox in the human being, and the colt having passed through it, the constitution seems to have undergone a purification and improvement. In some instances it has affected the animal in so mild a form that it has passed through its various stages, and gone off without much inconvenience to it, or any remedial means being employed. Contagion seems to have nothing to do with this disorder: every horse has this complaint once in its life and only once.

This, like many more complaints, commences with the animal coughing, and differs but little from a common cough, and is often mistaken for it in its early stages. It, however, differs from common catarrh by a more abundant discharge from the nostrils, which is of a yellowish colour, and unaccompanied by any disagreeable smell; it is also in most cases mixed with matter. There is, besides, a profuse discharge of slimy stringy fluid from the mouth. The membrane lining of the nose is intensely red. It will be found that a considerable swelling has taken place between the jaws, accompanied by fever, which is distinguished by want of appetite, a quick pulse, and a hot mouth, with a general weakness of the whole frame producing a dejected appearance. There is likewise a quick motion of the flanks and a coldness of the legs and ears. The swelling is in the form of a tumour between the jaws, increasing with various degrees of rapidity, occupying in some instances the whole of the space between the jaws, giving great pain to the horse while eating; it besides manifests a great disinclination to feed. This is accompanied by much thirst, but the swelling prevents him drinking, and having drank a mouthful or two it desists, after which, and even after eating, it is frequently seized with a spasmodic cough with suffocating symptoms. The swelling is of one uniform body, and therefore differs from the swelling of the glands in common catarrh and the glanders. As the principal source of this complaint consists in the swelling between the jaws, the first thing to be attended to is to bring the tumour to a suppuration. The first thing to be done is to apply a sharp blister over the tumour between the jaws, and for this purpose use Stevens' blister, or biniodide of mercury. This administered in time will facilitate the discharge a week or two sooner than it would otherwise take place if allowed to come to a period naturally. It will also have a tendency to draw out the inflammation from the mucous membrane of the throat, and consequently greatly ameliorate the cough. The old practice of fomenting and applying poultices to the tumour has almost passed away, as they often proved ineffectual from the great thickness of the horse's skin. Shortly after the blister has been applied, a hot linseed meal poultice may be added, and repeated twice a day until the tumour has become full of matter and is quite soft. The tumour frequently breaks of its own accord, but I do not like to do so as the lips of the wound in that case become jagged, and take a longer time to heal. I prefer to take a lancet and insert it in the bottom of the tumour and cut upwards, making a cut an inch or an inch and a-half in length. The matter must be well squeezed out, and the lips of the incision kept open with a piece of lint, which should be kept in the wound for at least a week to keep up the suppuration, otherwise a second tumour may be formed which frequently proves very difficult to cure. After the matter has been discharged, a small quantity of carbolised oil may be injected into the wound daily. At this stage of the complaint, if there is no unusual degree of fever, it is advisable to give a laxative, and the following will be found very good for

L

the purpose :—Barbadoes aloes two drachms, Castile soap one drachm, common salt four ounces, water one pint. If there is much fever with difficult breathing, proceeding from an affection of the chest, it will be necessary to resort to aconite in ten-drop doses. Old veterinary surgeons used to bleed for this complaint, but the writer is inclined to think that it does more harm than good, as it has a tendency to retard suppuration, and in this complaint all our efforts are to promote abundant suppuration.

Cooling medicine will be found of great benefit in this complaint, and two or three doses of the following will be found very beneficial :—Nitre one ounce, tartar emetic two drachms. If there is no fever the animal will soon manifest a desire to eat, and his food should chiefly be oatmeal gruel, bran mashes, and green food if it can be obtained. Should these not keep the bowels sufficiently open, which is of great consequence in this complaint, then the above laxative must be given, which will have the effect of preventing eruptions, which often occur after this complaint, and nothing more will be required if it operates freely. If, however, the complaint is followed by weakness it will be necessary to have recourse to tonic medicine, which should be repeated daily, until the horse has recovered strength. The following is a beautiful tonic :—Quinine twenty grains, gentian two drachms, calomel two drachms, ginger two drachms; this should be made into a ball and given every day. In bad cases of strangles, the parotid gland will swell to a great size, and even become ulcerated, and in other cases an accumulation of fluid will take place from the swelling of the duct, and cause the vessel to burst; in this event a fistulous ulcer will follow, which will be found very difficult to eradicate. In such a case it will be necessary to call in the aid of a practical veterinary surgeon, as an operation must be had recourse to which can only be performed by an experienced and practical veterinary surgeon. Strangles seem incidental to the horse in all countries, and foreign veterinary surgeons conceived the idea of innoculating to produce a milder degree of this disease, which they performed with either part of the discharge of the nostril or matter from the tumour; in many cases this had a most beneficial result, being both shorter in its duration and milder in its results, but English practitioners seem to entirely neglect this.

CANKER IN THE MOUTH.

It is but a too common occurrence for the mouth of a horse to become wounded by the bit, which may be too acute at its edges or fit badly, and often I am sorry to say by rough usage from both groom and master. It is no uncommon occurrence to see a so-called gentleman, if his horse is a little skittish, pull at its mouth with a sharp bit with sudden jerks, or saw its mouth from side to side with a sharp twisted bit; this treatment frequently wounds deeply, especially between the grinders and tusk where the bit rests, and it is no uncommon occurrence for the entire flesh to be torn off. The writer has had cases where the jawbone has been injured and pieces of the bone splintered off, and done by men who would be shocked at the idea of not being considered

Christian gentlemen, and who would be quite ready to punish severely any slight act of cruelty done by an ignorant drover. It may be easily conceived the great pain this causes to the poor animal, and those who have had the slightest touch of inflammation of the gums will have some idea of its sufferings. Every man with any feeling will make it his first study to see that the bit fits the horse, does not hurt its mouth, and can in no way injure the sides of the mouth or the palate. Even his own comfort ought to dictate this, as no horse can perform its work pleasantly while it is suffering from an irritation of the mouth. When the owner or groom finds the bone injured he should at once send for a veterinary surgeon, as it may be necessary to perform an operation to remove the shattered portions of the bone, but if the wounds are only of a fleshy nature they may be cured by the parts being frequently washed with alum, one ounce to one quart of water. If the wound has become ulcerated it may be necessary to touch the parts affected with lunar caustic or liquid nitrate of silver, to stimulate and cause them to heat ; at the same time the wash is being used it will be proper to give a laxative such as has been recommended for farcy. This complaint is one that could be entirely prevented by a little care and patience on the part of the rider or driver, yet we often see men pull at the sensitive mouth of a horse as if they had a bull by the horns, and this frequently happens from some fault of their own. The horse may be nervous and shy at some object it does not thoroughly understand, when, instead of a gentle word and a slight pull of the head in an opposite direction, down comes the whip or in go the spurs, when the animal plunges forward, and is then met with a chop in the mouth with the bit and pinched underneath with the curb, or sawn from side to side if driven with a snaffle. No man should " saw " a horse unless it is in the act of running away.

DISEASES OF THE TEETH OF HORSES.

Very little is known about the teeth of the horse as far as regards their diseases, yet the writer is we convinced that the horse, like man, often suffers con siderably by disease of the teeth. Many horses have come under his observation that were reduced to mere skeletons through bad teeth. This is a part of veterinary work that is often overlooked when examining a horse, and many horses are physicked and drenched with medicine for imaginary complaints of the liver, when with a little careful examination the evil would be found to be the result of a hollow tooth. Horses that have bad teeth generally have a dull, heavy appearance, frequently taking a mouthful of hay or corn and partly chewing it, then let it drop ; they will open their mouth and move the tongue about from side to side, and let the corn fall out as if they had got a stone in with the corn. It is not often that rot takes place, from the fact that the constant use of the grinders in chewing grain or straw wears them down to their natural form, yet many horses are found by that same practice with their teeth as sharp as a lance on the edges, and the edges worn unevenly. This cuts the inside of the cheek or the tongue, to prevent which the teeth should be filed down. If from the above cause the cheek or tongue has been cut, and an ulcer formed, the mouth should be washed with alum and water, as much alum being used as the water will dissolve. Sometimes the teeth grow irregularly in length, more especially the grinders; this proceeds generally from their not being immediately opposite each other. Instances are not wanting where the teeth have grown an inch or more above the general level of the grinders. Indeed, the writer lately had a case of this sort at Wellbury, and it became necessary to cut away above an inch of the tooth, to enable the animal to grind its corn. Horses often fall out of condition from these causes, therefore it becomes the careful groom to look well to his horse's teeth. If the horse is off its feed, try and find the cause; it is often that the teeth are either decayed or have met with an injury, or become rough at the edge. Some years ago the writer had a horse which fell off its feed, and he could find no cause for it, until he examined its mouth, when, to his surprise, he found a hollow tooth, and a lath nail sticking fast in the tooth up to its head. The nail must have been in the corn, and in eating it become fast embedded in the hollow tooth. He extracted the nail with great difficulty, and afterwards punched out the tooth, and never had any more trouble with the horse. Another subject of decayed teeth came under his care in 1874; it was a bay gelding, six years old, and was in very bad condition when brought. Upon carefully examining the mouth, it had six hollow teeth in the top jaw, four incisor and two molar teeth, and upon cleaning out the teeth, he found oats that had sprouted to the extent of a quarter of an inch. He cleaned all the teeth out and then filled the cavities with warm gutta-percha, and smoothed the surface with a hot iron; after this the horse fed well and soon got into good condition, and remained so for two years afterwards. The writer occasinally looked to the teeth, and if any of the gutta-percha fell out he replaced it. When horses are out of condition from bad teeth it is always advisable to put them through a course of medicine, as they often suffer from indigestion consequent upon swallowing food in an unmasticated state, and for this purpose nothing is better than that recommended earlier in this work for canker in the mouth. The lips of the horse are often lacerated and become sore by the smallness of the bit, or by the unmerciful rough hands of the rider or driver, and also from the shortness of the snaffle. Some people are foolish enough to gag the horse with the snaffle, and will give as an excuse for such cruel treatment that they do not like to see the bridle hang loosely on the horse's head. This wretched system often results in the horse having sores at the angle of the mouth, and sometimes poll-evil is the result of their foolish fashion. The severe excoriation of these parts produces deep ulcers, which cannot be removed while the animal is at work. Washing the mouth with alum and water is the best curative which we know; if the sore becomes callous, it may be necessary to touch the sides of the wound with nitrate of silver. Few persons are aware of the very great importance of the lips of the horse; they are the same to the horse as hands are to man. Without their aid it could not collect its food in the field, nor even convey the corn down its throat. To prove this the writer will give an account of an experiment which was tried with an ass, to ascertain the extent of the use of these important organs. The nerves which give feeling and sensation to the lips were divided, and instantly it was perceived that it was not aware when it touched its food with them. They were entirely divested of motion, and it was in consequence unable to convey the oats with which its manger was filled to his teeth, and by hunger it made a violent effort to lick up a few with its tongue, but they were nearly all rubbed off before they could be conveyed to its mouth.

THE EYE

of the horse is certainly the most important organ possessed by that animal, yet how little we know of it with its multitude of nerves and muscles. We frequently meet with cases of disease of the eye which are a great trouble to cure. The most common is inflammation, which generally makes its appearance unexpectedly, accompanied by considerable swelling of the eyelids, partially closing them, and causes a discharge of watery matter or tears. The lids exhibit inflammation, and some of the vessels of the eyeball are gorged with blood ; there will also be a dimness in the cornea. This usually accompanies a catarrh, but is also caused by substances getting into the eye, such as a hay seed, or it may be the result of a blow. When inflammation occurs, the eye should be carefully examined to ascertain if any foreign substance has got into it, and the true case discovered. This seldom affects the health of the horse, or prevents its feeding. After examining the eye, it should be bathed with warm water for half an hour, then bathed with the following :—Tincture of opium half an ounce water one pint ; or the following is equally as good :— Powdered leaves of foxglove one ounce, boiling water one quart. It is always advisable to give mashes for food, and mild doses of physic. Three or four days should be enough to remove this complaint. If it does not, you may infer that instead of common inflammation you have a case of opthalmia, and should call in the aid of the veterinary surgeon, as it will, if not properly treated in its first stages, end in total blindness. Opthalmia is manifested by great inflammation in the eyelids as well as in the cornea, and a watery humour and iris, all of which assume a dim appearance, and lose their transparency. The animal can hardly open its eyelids from the pain produced by exposure to the light. This disease is extremely difficult to combat, and after a month's constant treatment the eye will exhibit an alternation of remission and increase of inflammation day after day. One day it will have all the appearance of being nearly well, and on the next exhibit more unfavourable symptoms than it has before assumed. The gorged appearance of the inner membrane of the eyelid will be much abated, and the inflammation on the white of the eyeball will have nearly quitted it, the hazy aspect of the cornea will have assumed a certain degree of clearness, and to all appearance the malady will have taken its departure. This appearance is deceptive; it is only the lull before the storm ; it seldom happens that it is gone, for in six weeks or two months we too frequently find the eye again affected with all its former redness, and often worse than on the first attack. Sometimes both eyes are affected ; indeed, from time to time a succession of these abatements and attacks will have succeeded one another until a cloudy appearance and permanent opacity of the lens or capsule of the eye has taken place, and confirmed blindness in one or both eyes has resulted.   The cause of this complaint is to be looked for in bad ventilation of stables.   The constantly heated air of the stable may be considered the remote cause of this disease, to which all horses seem to be predisposed.   The poisoned air is a powerful agent in propagating ophthalmia, yet how few pay any regard to their ventilation, and what are generally considered the best stables are oftentimes the worst ventilated.   To this may be added the too frequent use of stables which are totally dark, so that when the animal is suddenly brought to the light, the abrupt transition produces spasmodic effect on the muscles and vessels of the eye, and causes that excessive inflammation which accompanies this disease.   When this disease first makes its appearance, the inside of the eyelids should be freely lanced, which often has the effect of stopping the complaint.   The horse should be put upon low diet, and gentle purgative medicine given. Bleeding at the temporal artery has often been beneficial in diseases of the eye.   When the cornea presents a cloudy appearance, bleeding and cooling medicine are most likely to relieve it, after which use some exciting means to give energy to the absorbents, and for this purpose nothing is better than corrosive sublimate in solution, two grains in an ounce and a-half of water will be found quite strong enough. This should be syringed into the eye twice or three times a day. If opacity of the lens has taken place we are not aware of anything that will remove it, indeed it is a given fact amongst the veterinary surgeons of note that no cure has been found, yet it is always advisable to call in the aid of the veterinary surgeon in diseases of the eye, for although they are few in number they are of vital consequence, as the least mistake in the treatment terminates in total blindness.

THE HAW.

It is not an unusual thing for a thickening of this part of the eye to take place, and protrude on the fore part of the eyeball; in this disease the retractor muscle pulls back the eye to protect it from the irritating effect of the light, and the thickening of the haw pushes it forward, and in consequence of the adjacent parts being thickened no retraction can take place. In former times the old veterinary surgeons used to cut out the haw of the eye, but that cruel, useless, and absurd practice is now abandoned by the enlightened veterinary surgeon, who knows the use of the haw of the eye of the horse, and allows Nature's handiwork to remain intact. Nature evidently intended the haw of the eye to protect the eye from dust and insects. The horse has no hands to take out dust or insects that may get into the eye, so Nature provided him with the haw, which it can draw over the eye at pleasure, and remove any dust or insect that may have lodged there. In former times few farriers understood the use of the haw, and even yet it is surprising the amount of ignorance displayed by many who ought to know better, but yet cannot tell of what value it is to the horse· In cases of inflammation of the eye it sometimes becomes much inflamed and increased in dimensions, and the contiguous parts likewise thickened. This sometimes forces it out of its place, but mostly it is voluntarily produced to protect the eye from the action of the light. In some cases it does not return into its place, and has been mistaken for a tumour or extraneous excrescence, and has been cut out by ignorant persons, and the eye consequently left unguarded.

In some instances where inflammation has a long continuation, ulceration of the haw and the destruction of the cartilage ensue. If the above does not stop the ulceration, then the following must be used :—White vitriol half an ounce, water three ounces ; and if it becomes callous, a weak solution of nitrate of silver should be applied to it, but in any case it is much better for a practical veterinary surgeon to be called in, as a mistake is easily made, and the result is a blind horse.

ERUPTIONS OF THE EYELIDS.

This irritating complaint is very common to the horse, and consists of a scale-like eruption. This is always attended with great itching, which causes the horse to rub its eyelid on the stall, or anything it comes in contact with, in the performance of which the animal often injures the eye itself. The edges of the eyelids should be anointed with the following ointment, which, after two or three applications will invariably effect a cure :—Hog's lard half an ounce, beeswax half an ounce, nitrated ointment of mercury half an ounce.

WARTS.

These are ofttimes a troublesome thing on the eyelid, and indeed on any part of the horse. Many different modes are resorted to to take them away, such as tying a piece of silk tightly round them and allowing them to rot off, but the quickest, most simple, and effective, is to take a pair of sharp scissors and cut them off close to the skin. Then touch the roots with nitrate of silver or lunar-caustic, and they will heal up in a few days and cease to trouble. They seldom come again when once cut off and caustic is applied.

GUTTA SERENA.

This is another disease of the eye which happily is not often met with, and exhibits itself by an extraordinary dilation of the pupil, which becomes immovable and has a bright glassy appearance. This is caused by a paralysis of the optic nerve, or the surface of the retina, or what is often called the mirror of the eye, occasioned by a determination of blood to the brain, and its consequent pressure on the optic nerve thus destroying its functions. Cures in this disease are very rare ; indeed I doubt if any well-authenticated cases really exist. Of the three cases which have come under my observation during the past

15 years, neither of them were cured, although bleeding, medicine, the rowel and seton were tried, and from the nature of the disease I have but little faith in all I have read as to a cure having been effected in a single confirmed case of gutta serena or glass eye.

GENERAL BLINDNESS AND IMPERFECT VISION.

No subject is of greater importance than the state of the organs of vision of the horse, which ought to occupy the first attention of a purchaser. Blindness or a partial defect of the eyes often leads to many unpleasant consequences to the proprietor, whether he is riding or driving. It requires considerable knowledge of the anatomical construction of the eye to enable anyone to judge correctly of its perfection or defects; and I am sorry to say that not half of the members of the veterinary profession pay due attention to the eye, and do not make it so much of a study as should be devoted to it. We have many disputes about the eye of the horse; one in particular occurred at a recent show at Islington, where Professor Pritchard disqualified the winner of the first prize in consequence of cataract in the eye. This is one of the most difficult diseases of the eye for a practical man to detect, and unless the practitioner is himself blessed with good eyesight, and has been taught by a thoroughly practical man how to stand, and how to place the horse's eyes to the light, the chances are that he will pass the horse as sound while it is in fact suffering from imperfect vision. When living in the neighbourhood of Hitchin, my employer had

a horse that he had hunted for some years, yet this
horse had as bad a cataract in the near eye as any
horse I ever saw that was not blind with it. This
horse was passed as sound, and the owner never
knew that the animal had a bad eye, yet to a minute
observer of small things the horse told instantly,
upon going up to it on its near side, that its vision
was impaired with that eye, as it always held its
head from you if approached on the near side, and
did not do so if approached on the off side. Dealers
in horses know well what a cataract is, and are
always anxious, if the horse has a defect in the eye,
to bring it at once into a strong light, so that the
purchaser or the examiner may be unable to detect
this disease. The cause of cataract is, in most instances, from inflammation, or the result of a blow ;
this causes a light cloudy appearance of the retina,
which cannot be seen unless the examiner brings
the horse out gradually from the dark to the light, and
places his own face to the cheek of the horse and looks
stedfastly into its eye, and watch minutely the contraction of the pupil when brought to the light. The
examiner should be very careful and observe if both eyes
contract alike, or if in the retina there is a dull blueish
white appearance ; if there is, the chances are that the
horse has imperfect vision, if not cataract. Indepen-
dently of the beauty of a prominent eye, it is of much
importance that the cornea should possess considerable
convexity, but this must have a limit. If very
prominent, the rays of light will be too convergent,
which will cause indistinct vision, and the animal

will prick its ears forward and look at any object it is about to pass in a nervous manner, being unable to determine what the object may be. Thoughtless drivers will whip the horse for this, causing the animal to have two fears to contend with instead of one; its indistinct vision makes it fear passing objects, and being nervous at the object it also expects the whip, will start suddenly on one side and then set off at a gallop. On the other hand, if the cornea be flat and small the rays may not be sufficiently convergent, and consequently will render the vision imperfect, and as it cannot see distinctly it will suddenly stop upon coming unawares upon any object it does not understand, and in all probability bolt round to the danger of the rider or driver's neck. A horse is unsafe with either of these defects, both in riding and driving. The cornea should therefore be moderately convex, perfectly transparent, and totally free from all opacity or cloudiness over its entire surface. As I have said before, the best method of examining the eye of the horse is to place the cheek of the scrutinizer close to the cheek of the horse, both behind and under the eye. The latter position is the most advantageous to see it thoroughly. The open air is not favourable for the examiner (hence dealers knowing the horse has defective vision are always anxious to bring them out to the light). The head of the horse should be a little within the door of the stable, and by looking outwards, any defect is rendered more visible. If any faint, whitish, milk-like streaks be noticed passing over the cornea, it is

certain the animal has had inflammation in that
portion of the eye; but should the centre part of the
cornea be perfectly transparent, and yet the margin of
it where it unites with the sclerotica have a hazy ring,
it may be concluded that this has been occasioned by
recent inflammation, and consequently the eye is predisposed to a return of it. During the operation of
thus inspecting the eye, mind that no white or pale-
coloured object be near, as its form and great transparency are very likely to reflect these rays, and
deceive the person making the examination. Attention to the dilation and contraction of the pupil will
materially aid a person in the detection of blindness
or otherwise. When the cornea and crystalline lens
are quite transparent, with the retina paralysed and of
course not liable to be affected with the light, it is
extremely difficult to detect blindness either in one or
both eyes. It generally happens that when a horse is
totally blind, he has a constant and rapid motion
with its ears, it also lifts its feet high as if some
obstacle presented itself, and puts its feet down
with cautious uncertainty. Do not forget to pay
particular attention to the pupil of both eyes, and
notice if they are both of a size while it is in the stable,
and as it approaches the door observe whether both
pupils contract equally as they are subjected to a
stronger light. If, however, the horse is in a fair or at a
distance from a stable, place the crown of a black hat
over the eye, and then observe after it has obscured it
from the light for a little while whether the pupils contract. Repeat the experiment on both eyes, and you will

M

be able to judge if both present the same appearance.
Dishonest dealers and horse-copers will not like you to
examine their horses minutely, but as my writing is for
the instruction of my readers and for the younger members of my profession, I shall still continue to point out
the tricks of the " professional " horse-coper, as a guide
and warning to all who may want to buy a horse, not
caring for the discomfort of the few if I can benefit the
many.   Being " proud to praise yet not afraid to blame "
is a motto I hold by, and in future pages I will devote a
chapter or two upon the tricks of horse-copers, so that
my readers may then see it is not a wonder that many
persons are deceived when buying a horse, the only
wonder being that any escape who have any dealings
with them.   Before leaving the horse's head, there is one
disease I must not overlook, viz.,

POLL-EVIL.

This disease consists of an inflammation of the
muscles of the neck over the poll-bone, and the first
vertebra of the neck.   It generally extends under the
ligament of the neck, which passes over the atlas-bone.
This ligament is not attached to the bone, consequently
the disease is deep-seated, being situate between that
ligament and the bone itself.   It is being thus deep-
seated which frequently renders it difficult to cure, the
bone itself being frequently diseased before suppuration
is set up.   Before the swelling becomes very conspicuous,
the part is very hot and painful to the touch, which can
easily be noticed by the motion of the horse.   That it
has all the painfulness of a whitlow in the human

subject, the symptoms fully bear out, therefore those who have had a whitlow on their finger will have some sympathy for the horse when suffering from poll-evil. This disease is the result of a blow on the head between the ears, often caused by leading the horse out of low stable doors, when the horse will at times throw up. its head and strike it upon the door-frame with great force. If this is not attended to at the time, the blood becomes congealed, suppuration sets in, the matter finds its way between the bone and muscles, and a deep sloughing wound is the result before it is fully recognised by the owner. Sometimes this is the result of a blow given by an unmerciful rider, at other times it is brought on by the horse striking its head upon the under-part of the manger; it is also often brought on by the ligaments being stretched by that horrible piece of torture, a tight bearing-rein; but from whatever cause the malady proceeds, it is frequently exceedingly troublesome and tedious to cure. If noticed before suppuration takes place, every means should be adopted to suppress the inflammation, and if possible to disperse the swelling. Medicine of a laxative kind should be given, and hot fomentations should be constantly applied, afterwards a piece of sponge or linen cloth should be placed upon the part affected, and kept constantly wet with arnica lotion, one part arnica (British proof) to forty of pure spring water. If the swelling remains hard for two or three days in spite of the above treatment, then use strong tincture of iodine; this should be painted upon the part with a soft brush, and will frequently take away the swelling by absorption. If it is found that the swelling continues in spite of this treatment, then other means must be resorted to, and applications to facilitate the ripening of the tumour must be adopted. This is best effected by poultices of hot linseed meal, warm fomentations, and dressing with stimulating oils, such as soap liniment or Elliman's embrocation, or, what is better still, Gregory's Vesico Sudorific. Care must, however, be taken not to allow suppuration to break out of its own accord, as this will leave a very ugly sore, and the wound will be long healing. The progress of the disease must be very narrowly watched, and when the tumour becomes soft to the touch it must be opened with a lancet and afterwards kept open with a seton. A needle with the cord attached must penetrate the apex of the tumour, and be brought out a little way below the tumour, and the incision with the lancet should be large to allow of free suppuration, for if the matter cannot run freely away it will set up a great amount of irritation. Gentle pressure must be used to squeeze all the matter out of the wound, after which nothing more will be required for three or four days. After the seton has set up a healthy reaction, which may be known by the matter discharged being of a light straw colour and of the thickness of thick cream, the seton may be removed, and the wound dressed with carbolized oil, five oil to one acid. It may be necessary to divide the ligaments of the neck with the lance to expose the bottom of the abscess to the action of the acid, but no evil effects will result from this, as both ends of the ligaments will unite again in a few days. It often happens that the wound will fill too rapidly with new

flesh when using carbolized oil, and it may be necessary
to touch the parts with nitrate of silver or lunar caustic
to consolidate the parts. This is a good omen; but
should this treatment not have the effect of setting up a
healthy condition, then it will be necessary to call in
the aid of a practical veterinary surgeon, for in all
probability the bones of the neck are fractured, and as
these can only be successfully treated by a practical
man it is useless giving my readers the mode adopted.
The cord of the seton should be dressed every morning
with carbolized oil or corrosive sublimate half a
drachm, spirit of wine two ounces, but in most cases
carbolized oil is best. Setons are largely employed in
the management of domesticated animals in disease
and even in health. They consist of pieces of tape or
cord, which are carried for some distance under the
skin and allowed to remain in a considerable time to
keep the passage open for the draining away of some
morbid product, or to establish some curative or
prophylactic process by the local irritation which they
produce. The word seton is no doubt obtained from
the Latin *seta*, coarse hair or bristles, which were the
original agents for this purpose; at the present time
the material in common use is coarse tape varying
according to the requirements of the case or the whim
of the operator. It is introduced by means of an instrument called the seton needle, and is formed of
a flat piece of steel varying from four to eight inches
in length. The one end has a square aperture or eye,
while the other end is flattened out at the edges which
join each other at an acute angle. The point is often

made sharp to allow of its being pushed through the skin ; sometimes, however, it is left blunt, and it is then passed through the skin by an opening made with a lancet. They are often used with a handle, into which they are screwed, and in this way their course is more certainly directed. In introducing a seton the skin is first punctured transversely with a lancet, and the seton needle is directed between the skin and muscles, its course being favoured by the pulling out of the skin by the left hand in front of the point of the instrument. It is usually carried from a point above downward to permit of a free discharge of the matter, and when carried far enough a fresh incision is made with the lancet to allow of its exit. This is preferable to penetrating the skin simply with a sharp needle, as the wounds thus made are often so small that the pus cannot escape freely, and becoming imprisoned produces a source of irritation. The seton having been introduced, it is necessary to fix it by some means ; the most common way of doing this is to tie both ends together, but this is objectionable, as the animal may by rubbing get the loop fast and tear it out, leaving an ugly tear. The best way is to make a large knot at each end of the tape, which should be about four inches longer than the wound on each end, so that the matter can be worked out by pulling the cord up and down. In spavin and various other forms of lameness they are at times employed with great benefit in the neighbourhood of the malady. Their effect is sometimes increased by smearing the seton with an irritant such as a preparation of black hellebore, turpentine, iodine, euphorbium, &c. A peculiar system sometimes employed successfully in spavin is the introduction of a thread, medicated in this way, deeply into the soft parts over the seat of the bony tumour. This is chiefly recommended by the fact that if well managed it leaves no bluish marks on the hock.

SORE BACKS.

In most cases these are attributable to two causes, ignorance and a want of cleanliness. The skin of the horse is subject to many diseases, and is very sensitive ; the cuticle or outer skin is often subject to injury through careless and ill-fitting harness, especially cart saddles, which are the chief cause of bad backs, coupled with unskilful loading. Everyone knows that it is necessary to load a cart forward to enable a horse to draw a load up-hill ; but how few do we see who shift the load backward when the horse has to go down-hill. The carters in Scotland are very particular in these matters, and when carrying stone from quarries will always have some large stones which they can move to balance the load. Another thing they always use, plenty of grease to the backband or chain which runs through the saddle, to enable it to run easily through, as the shafts vibrate from side to side over the inequalities of the road. These things are often neglected, especially in Kent, and consequently the load, bearing with undue weight upon the horse's back, and the backband not being greased, every time the cart vibrates the saddle rocks upon the horse's back. The constant friction sets up inflammation of the cuticle, which closes the pores of the true skin, and prevents a healthy perspiration, and causes small pustules. These are aggravated by continual pressure, and the irritation is kept up by the rocking of the saddle. An abscess forms, breaks, and ultimately becomes a bad back. Here want of cleanliness becomes a tyrant; as no attention is paid to the lining of the saddles, sweat accumulates, and the lining becomes as hard as a board. Some horses are more liable to sore backs than others; but a little care will always prevent them becoming ulcerated. The first thing which should be done when a horse has chafed his back is to wash it clean with warm water and soda, *not soft soap*, and afterwards apply strong salt and water, or, what is far better, a strong decoction of oak bark. This, with a day or two of rest, will be all that is required. But should the sore be of a deep nature, it will be necessary to dress the parts with carbolic acid one part, sweet oil seven parts, which, with rest to the part afflicted, will cure it in a few days. Sore shoulders are caused by the same neglect of cleanliness and badly fitting collars, and require the same treatment.

ROARING.

This is a disease that is too well known in this country, yet, strange as it may appear, the Arab does not know of it in his stud ; and of the thousands of horses of that class that came under my observation, when buying horses for the Spanish Government, during the Don Carlos war, I do not recollect one that was affected as a roarer ; and the author is of opinion that the Arab and barb are free from this complaint, and no doubt our climate has something to answer for in this respect. This is a disease arising from an affection of the larynx and superior portion of the windpipe. When a horse so affected has been hard trotted or galloped, he may be heard at some distance to utter a grunting sound, or when he is standing if touched suddenly with a stick or whip he will grunt or groan. Dealers are often seen to lay hold of the horse by the head with the left hand, while with the right hand they feign to hit the horse; he will cringe away from them and utter a loud grunt if he is a roarer. This disease is supposed to be produced by a thickening of the larynx and upper portion of the windpipe, in consequence of previous inflammation, and thus obstructing the passage and limiting its action. After strangles this disease frequently follows, and it is a noticeable fact that horses whose sires or dams were affected with this disease are predisposed to the complaint. Another great cause of this complaint, in the carriage or harness horse, is the cruel and absurd bearing-rein, which gags the horse's head out of its natural form, and the constant strain on the muscles of the neck set up inflammation in the region of the maxillary gland, the larynx becomes affected, thickening takes place, and for our foolish fashion, a horse that would have been worth a hundred guineas becomes fit only for a cab horse. By this action the larynx and superior muscles of the windpipe are circumscribed and ultimately become semi-paralysed with consequent loss of power and action; therefore the opening not being sufficiently capacious during the rapid breathing occasioned by violent exercise, the pressure of air rushing through the circumscribed space, the sound is produced (in much the same manner that a boy makes a noise through a lark-call) which has been absurdly called " roaring." The practice of what is termed *coughing* a horse to ascertain the state of his wind is apt to cause this complaint ; this is performed by subjecting the larynx or trachea to violent pressure by squeezing with the fingers. A horse so affected may be considered as decidedly unsound. In this disease there are little reliable remedies to be had ; blisters have given relief, but after a horse has once become a confirmed " roarer " nothing we can do will cure him. When, as it sometimes happens, this disease has been of the character to threaten suffocation, the part supposed to cause the difficulty of breathing by obstructing the passage of the air has been cut down upon, and a portion of one of the rings of the windpipe cut out and a breathing tube inserted. This is one of the first operations I ever recollect seeing my deceased father perform ; this was cutting a horse's throat to save its life.

INFLAMMATION OF THE LUNGS.

Of all the diseases incidental to the horse, there is none which we have more to dread than inflammation of the lungs ; it is the most prevalent, and at the same time the most fatal. Sometimes this disease comes on so suddenly that the horse is almost dead before the attack is discovered. Many horses are left at night to all appearances well, and in the morning are found either dead or dying from this disease, but in the greater number of cases fever is a premonitory symptom. In most case in the early stages of the disease it is not very rapid, but it is heavy in its action and indistinct, feeling vibratory under the pressure of the finger; in other cases it is hardly to be perceived, so languid is its motion. These are the cases that generally prove fatal, as many men do not understand this disease, and take no notice of it in its early stages, so that the attack assumes a violent form before remedies are administered. In many cases that have come under the author's observation, the horse has been noticed to be dull and off its feed for a day or two before anything was thought wrong. Such is the ignorance of many men, that they do not know that a horse is ill until it falls down at plough or in its harness, then they think there must be something the matter, and send for the veterinary surgeon, who often arrives in time to see the animal die, and he then gets the credit of not being able to save the horse. We often hear cases of this sort being talked about by those who have charge of horses. This disease in its early stages is not very rapid, and is followed by dilated nostrils, coldness in the extremities, and heaving at the flanks, which clearly indicate an oppression in the breathing, differing, however, from the hard laboured action of horses in fever, and also the irregular breathing of broken-winded horses, appearing as if two respirations were required for every inspiration of air to the lungs. In inflammation the pulse is quick, hurried, and irregular, caused by the pain which is felt by the animal at each attempt to draw in the air, giving the appearance of something being imperfect in the respiratory organs. The animal thrusts out its head, the mucous membrane of the nose becomes very red, especially in the inside angles of the nostrils, where it continues, although at times it extends further up, from which position it may disappear, but still maintains its chief position in the lower portion of the nostril. The animal expresses great anxiety in its look, and turns its head frequently and hurriedly round to its flanks, more especially to that side where the inflammation has settled. It stands in a straddling manner, with its fore legs generally apart; it seldom lies down, and when it does it is but for a few minutes, remaining for days on its legs. It does not, however, always happen that the premonitory systems are the same, for in many cases inflammation comes on slowly and in an insidious manner; perhaps the horse may be off its feed and its coat will stare, its breathing may be but slightly accelerated and abbreviated, with the legs a little colder than usual. Sometimes inflammation of the lungs is preceded by symptoms which are attendant upon common fever, catarrh, or the distemper. In such instances the true disease manifests itself in full force before the groom or master of the horse in the least suspect it. The first manifestations are coldness in the limbs and ears, accompanied by a hurried pulse and anxious look, with a seeming dread of lying down. This is soon followed by an irregularity and indistinctness of the pulse, and extreme coldness of the legs and ears. The nostrils become

livid and it scarcely seems to breathe; it grinds its
teeth, and this may be regarded as a certain symptom
of dissolution. Staggering ensues, and it finally
sinks in its stall. Sometimes if in a loose box or yard
it will continue to walk round and round in a circle,
with its head slightly sideways. If the left lung is
affected it will walk round on the right circle, always
keeping the left side on the outside of the circle, but
if the right lung is the seat of the attack it will walk
in a circle quite the reverse. When the horse begins
walking in this manner it is a bad sign, not one in
fifty ever recovering. This last is a picture of that
kind of inflammation that has lurked in the system
without exhibiting premonitory symptoms, and which
in most cases proves fatal. Again, there are cases in
which the disease is so rapid that it will have undergone its entire stages in twenty-four hours, and in
this short time the entire mass of the lungs will have
suffered complete destruction. Such a case has been
satisfactorily proved not to proceed from long and
deep-rooted inflammation, but assuredly from the
very reverse. It has been caused by the extraordinary degree of inflammation bursting the coating of
the vessels and filling the air-cells with blood, thus
instantly destroying their functions. There are bad
cases which are not so rapid in their termination, but
which are nevertheless equally fatal. This happens
when no rupture of the vessels has taken place, and
although means have been adopted to take off the
pressure of the inflammation, yet they have been
insufficient to produce the desired effect. In such a-

case the breath of the horse will be extremely disagreeable, with a running at the nostrils, and is a sure
indication that mortification has taken place in the
substance of the lungs, and that death will soon follow.
Inflammation of the lungs will be distinguished from
inflammation of the bowels by the pulse, in the latter
case being small and wiry, the mucous membrane of
the nose not being so red, and by pain in the belly,
which is indicated by kicking, pawing, stamping, &c.
This malady is brought on in most instances by the
numerous and sudden transitions from heat to cold,
and more often from cold to heat, to which most horses
are subjected.   They are, under the careless and
wanton folly of masters and grooms, often galloped or
otherwise over-heated and permitted to cool in the
open air or in the draught of a stable.   The stable
itself is often too hot, frequently from twenty to thirty
degrees above the atmosphere, and most stables are
but ill-ventilated, consequently the air is of an impure
kind, and being breathed over and over again, affects
the membrane which lines the cells of the lungs.   The
constant irritation from ammonia, which the horse is
compelled to breathe in a foul, ill-ventilated stable,
weakens the membrane of the lungs, hence the susceptibility of irritation and inflammation from breathing an atmosphere which is impregnated with
ammoniacal gas, generated by manure and urine.   It
is quite evident, from the dangerous nature of this
complaint, that the treatment must be immediate
and decisive, and as the disease is rapid, so also must
be the treatment, as every minute is of vast importance,

and the life or death of the animal depends upon the treatment first adopted. Although the first symptoms may be of a mild character, yet we have seen how rapid they become in their after-effects; to palliate this would be absurd, the iron must be struck while it is hot, and in this case we cannot hit too hard if we mean to defeat the enemy, therefore the first remedy is too clip off all the hair from the sides, mix mustard with turpentine and vinegar into a thin paste, rub this well into the sides from near the back all over the ribs, in a circle at least of eighteen inches in diamater ; the whole of the horse's chest and windpipe should be also subjected to the beneficial effects of counter irritation. In olden times farriers used to bleed freely for inflammation of the lungs, but it is seldom re-sorted to now. If the horse is costive, which is fre-quently the case in inflammation of the lungs, the first thing is to get its bowels open ; for this purpose (never give aloes in inflammation) the best purgative to give is three half-pints of linseed oil. Some give castor-oil, but that mild aperient in the human being is both uncertain and unsafe when administered to the horse. Instead of bleeding we resort to the use of digitalis, aconite, and acetate of ammonia. In the early stages of inflammation of the lungs, give digitalis one drachm morning and night. If the fever runs very high give belladonna in drachm doses, alternately with digitalis. If the pulse is high, up to 80 or 100, give aconite in ten-drop doses every quarter of an hour, enemas of warm soap and water, with two ounces of linseed oil, which should be given every half-hour until the bowels are freely open. It often happens that horses are known to be a little ill, and no notice is taken of them until inflammation has set in ; then the owner or groom does not known if it is inflammation of the lungs, bowels, or colic, in which case it is always safe under the circumstances to administer the following, which often has the effect of arresting what would otherwise have been a case of severe inflammation :—Warm ale one quart, ginger one ounce, powdered aniseed one ounce, and tincture of opium one ounce. After the mustard has been on from ten minutes to a quarter of an hour, it should be carefully washed off, and the sides wiped dry with a soft cloth; no good is attained by leaving the mustard on.

If the horse still continues to blow, the mustard must be repeated, as it is only by severe treatment that we can pull him through. Some veterinary surgeons use Spanish flies for blistering the sides, but this I do not like as the system absorbs the fly, and leaves bad effects afterwards. During the time the fever is at its height the blister will seldom rise, the internal excitement overcoming the external one, and a failure in its operation also accompanies exhaustion. In this case there is danger to be apprehended, and it is always by far the safest to use mustard and turpentine freely; they are more rapid in their effects, always handy to get, and can be repeated from time to time to keep up the excitement, and at the same time the inflammation can be kept down by means of digitalis and aconite. After the inflammation has subsided, cooling medicine must be given, and the following also until an intermediate state of the pulse has been attained :—

Nitre three drachms, emetic tartar one and a-half drachm, and digitalis one drachm. This medicine should be persisted in until the horse hangs its head and becomes half stupid, having a flow of saliva from its mouth. In less than twenty-four hours after this condition has been effected the disease will be found to have completely subsided. It is a great mistake in this complaint to suppose that the stable should be kept very close and warm, as the very cause which in a great measure operated remotely in inducing the disorder is again brought into play; rather keep warm clothing on the horse, which will have a tendency to keep up insensible perspiration. After this the horse should be well rubbed down, the legs in particular should have a smart application of the brush to set up a circulation, after which they should be well wrapped in flannel bandage to keep up the action; the rubbing should be repeated from time to time. The less the animal eats the better; corn should in no case be given; green food and mashes may be set before him, but this in only small quantities. If the oppression in breathing now subsides, heat be restored to the limbs, and the animal lies down, these are sure indications that the horse is better, and that the symptoms have abated. The strength and appetite will now gradually improve, but much caution must be exercised in not allowing the animal to take too much food, which might have the effect of inducing a return of the malady. Green food, or, if that cannot be had, bran mashes and oatmeal gruel, and a little sweet hay should compose its food, but to restore strength where much exhaustion prevails, tonic medicine should be given. The mildest should be first administered, and this

N

is camomile in doses of from one to two drachms; after a day or two following may be given:—Camomile two drachms, ginger two drachms, and gentian two grains. Should the animal continue to improve, the diet may be extended, and probably in three or four days it may have a small quantity of corn, which may be increased until its strength is restored. A clean, cool stable is the best means of preventing predisposition to diseases of the lungs, both of which should be scrupulously attended to. The heated air of a stable and the poisonous gas arising from dung and urine prove most injurious to the horse. Bad ventilation and bad drains have much to answer for.

LOCAL INFLAMMATION.

The symptoms of local inflammation are redness of the parts, heat, pains, and swelling. The redness is induced by the increased flow of blood through the vessels of the parts affected, in consequence of the increased action of the blood-vessels. The heat arises from the change gradually taking place in the flow of the blood passing from the arterial to the venous condition, so that if more blood be propelled through the capillaries, more heat will consequently be produced in that situation. Swelling is induced by the same means as the redness, viz., from a fluid being deposited in the contiguous substance, and pain must be the effect of distension and pressure produced, and the consequent disarrangement of the nerves of the parts affected. Inflammation of every kind is caused by an increased flow of blood through the vessels of the part affected; consequently the remedies must be to reduce the circulation

to its ordinary and healthy action; therefore if the
inflammation has located itself in any of the vital
organs, the remedies must be prompt and severe.
Bleeding from the nearest vein is often very beneficial
in reducing inflammation, but it must always
be borne in mind that bleeding only gives temporary
relief, and reduces the inflammation at the time,
and is sure to return again in all its virulence if
medicine be not given to keep it in check, therefore
aconite, belladonna, and digitalis should be given.
If fever is high give aconite; if the pulse is high,
hard, and full, give digitalis. If the eyes are much
dilated, belladonna is required. For instance, if the
eye is the subject of inflammation, the gorged vessels
should be scarified, which will have more effect than
bleeding from the jugular vein, especially, as I have
said before, if medicine is judiciously administered.
A quart of blood taken from the toe of a horse
suffering from acuter founder will have more effect
than four quarts taken from the neck. Old writers,
and, indeed, all the veterinary surgeons of the old
school, used to bleed in inflammation in every part,
from whatever cause. The use of such drugs as
are named above has to a great extent superseded
the use of the lance. Whenever it is considered
necessary to have recourse to blood-letting in cases
of local inflammation, the stream of blood should flow
freely; and to effect this the broad-shouldered lancet
should be used, so that the wound in the vein may
be ample. In whatever situation the inflammation
occurs, and blood-letting is resorted to, the bleeding

should be immediate and ample; and after bleeding, purgative medicine must next be administered, because the mucous membrane of the bowels and coating of the stomach are in most instances affected sympathetically by a deranged action in any other part of the system. Should this not be the case they may be otherwise irregular, which invariably increases all kinds of inflammation, and fever is induced more especially when there is much retention. In any case purging has the effect of lessening the quantity of blood, by removing from it the serous or watery portion, and by determinating the blood to the bowels. The pressure is necessarily removed from the inflamed vessels, as it is a law of the animal economy that where the circulation is directed to one set of vessels it proportionately diminishes the flow in other parts of the system. Purging, by producing languor and sickness, lessens the general excitement, and hence the pressure upon the circulation is circumscribed. In administering medicine in cases of internal inflammation much caution and consideration is required, because what would be beneficial in some cases may be prejudicial in others. Thus in inflammation of the lungs aloes may be given as a purgative, but in inflammation of the bowels it would be decidedly wrong, from its tendency to gripe, and even in inflammation of the lungs purgative medicine should not be given until after the inflammatory symptoms have abated. In external inflammation, great difference of opinion prevails as to the treatment; some recommend cold embrocations as the most proper mode of treatment, being most likely to allay the heat in the part, and there can be but little doubt but they will speedily lessen the heat, from the well-known principle that coloric has a strong tendency to equalize itself or to quit any substance that is surcharged with it, consequently by these appliances the increased temperature is reduced in the part inflamed. Thus when using arnica lotion in cases of external inflammation the effect will be considerably heightened by dissolving two ounces of nitre in a quart of lotion, which should be composed of one ounce of arnica b.p. to forty ounces of water. When nitre is used with the lotion it should be used as soon as fairly dissolved, the inflamed portion being completely exposed to the process of evaporation. Nitre has the effect of reducing the temperature of the lotion many degrees below its natural condition, but it is questionable whether permanent benefit is derived from cold applications in cases of inflammation. My own experience lead me to believe more in warm fomentations. Although not so grateful as cold ones to hot swellings, they will be found to produce better results, as they open the pores of the skin, and if applied as hot as the animal can endure, it will more readily take off the tension that has been produced by inflammatory swelling ; poultices will have much the same effect. Blisters have often been applied with great success in deep-seated inflammations, for by creating inflammation on the surface on the principle of counter-irritation, it will have the tendency to lessen it in other parts, as great inflammation cannot exist in two places close together at the same time.

PLEURISY.

This disease, which unhappily is too common, is entirely confined to inflammation of the pleura or membrane which lines the chest—hence its name—and has connection with the substance of the lungs. The pulse is hard, but not oppressed, the extremities are cold, although not so much so as in common inflammation, nor is the membrane of the nostril very red. If pressure on the side is applied the horse will express pain by a sharp grunt. The unwillingness of the horse to lie down will soon manifest itself in this as in violent inflammation of the lungs. This disease, like inflammation of the lungs, is generally caused by sudden transitions from heat to cold. In this complaint bleeding is generally adopted, followed by a course of sedative medicine, administered in the form of a gentle purgative, which may be given with more safety in this disease than in inflammation of the lungs. If pleurisy is violent, it frequently induces dropsy in the chest, which, having no means of escape, lodges itself in the cavity of the chest. When this is the case little good is to be expected from the animal, and it is very seldom that a cure can be effected. Sometimes the chest is punctured for it, which has the effect of carrying off the fluid; but it too frequently happens that it is an ineffectual remedy. Whenever it is suspected that water is forming, puncturing should be had recourse to, the opening to be made by an instrument called the *trochar.* The cavity where it is inserted is the intercostal membrane between the seventh and eighth rib, and as close to the cartilage as possible. Diuretic medicine in combination with tonics should be administered. The following should be given :—Turpentine one ounce, ginger half a drachm, and linseed meal half an ounce; this to be made into a ball with syrup or treacle. Some prefer resin instead of turpentine. When attended with fever aconite and digitalis may be given, but a veterinary surgeon should be called in.

INFLAMMATION OF THE BOWELS.

The intestines are subject to two different kinds of inflammation, namely, that of mucous membrane or internal lining of the gut; the second is in the external coating of the bowels. These are very different in their character, and consequently in their mode of treatment. Inflammation of the mucous membrane is accompanied with violent purging, too often from overdoses of physic being administered, or from acid generated in the bowels by a bad quality of food, or from other unknown causes. In addition to purging, considerable pain attends this disease, which is indicated by the animal looking round at its flanks, with a heaviness in its breathing, accompanied by quick, feeble pulse, and hot mouth, ears, and legs. This is a complaint mostly met with in high-fed horses, as indeed are most cases of inflammation. High feeding has a tendency to induce inflammation. The sudden exposure of high-fed animals to a warm from a cold atmosphere, and being allowed to drink plentifully of cold water when in a heated condition, or having their bellies and legs wetted when in an overheating condition, are all causes that induce this complaint. This is a point in the management of the stable that the groom should never overlook. The horse should upon no account have a quantity of water given it directly after a hard journey; one quart of water is quite enough until the animal has had some corn or sweet hay, then more water and more food may be given with safety. Again, in washing the horse it is always better to let the dirt remain on than to wash it and not rub it perfectly dry. Many owners of horses will not allow their horses to be washed after a hard run with the hounds, upon the ground of preventing the chances of inflammation. It is not the washing that induces it so much as the neglect of rubbing dry. When this complaint is accompanied by excessive purging with great pain, astringent medicine should not be administered. All kinds of food should be denied it, and in its stead give gruel, a decoction of linseed, thin starch or arrowroot, and a strong solution of gum-arabic; clysters of warm gruel should also be given, in which a quarter of an ounce of aloes is mixed. Some prefer from six ounces to half-a-pound of Epsom salts. These should be administered with the clyster-pipe; Reid's patent pump is by far the best, but a good and cheap pipe can be made of a piece of elder and an ox-bladder. Take a piece of elder about a foot long, and after taking out the pith, tie the bladder on one end, and pour your gruel into the bladder, then force the stick of elder up the rectum and withdraw gently, the suction will nearly empty the bladder. If the irritation and continuation of pain continue after twelve or fourteen hours have elapsed, it will be necessary to give the following gruel in two quarts :—Prepared chalk one ounce, catechu four ounces, opium two scruples. This should be repeated every four hours until the purging

and pains are allayed, after which the doses should
be lessened in quantity, and given at greater intervals.
If the inflammatory symptoms are very great, it may be
necessary to blister the belly and sides with mustard,
and in extreme cases recourse must be had to bleeding,
but this must only be resorted to when accompanied
with general febrile symptoms. The horse must be kept
well clothed, and its legs thoroughly rubbed and bandaged. The next disease of the bowels is

SPASMODIC COLIC.

This disorder generally comes on very suddenly,
without any premonitory signs. The horse becomes
very restless, shifts his position, paws the ground, and
looks round at its flanks with great anxiety, sometimes
raising its foot as high as its belly, and strikes it
violently. It will also lie down and roll about on its
back ; in a few minutes the spasm will subside,
and the animal after shaking will resume feeding;
at longer or shorter intervals the attack is renewed,
but with increased violence, when it will throw itself
on the ground with considerable force, will break into a
copious perspiration, and heave greatly at the flanks.
The spasms are renewed at intervals, and gradually
become less frequent and less severe, or if on the contrary
they are more frequent and acute, and at length manifest an almost uninterrupted series, then it may be
suspected that violent inflammation and mortification
have taken place, and that death will speedily ensue.
Stones and large earthy lumps in the intestines cause
colic pains, but we cannot tell why they are present.

Drinking cold water when over-heated is frequently a cause of this complaint ; green food is also apt to induce these pains. Worms and bots are frequently the cause of spasms. A combination of opium and turpentine is a valuable specific in this disorder, in the following quantities :—turpentine three ounces, laudanum one ounce, warm ale one pint, or the following, which the writer prefers :—Spirit of pimento half-ounce, laudanum one ounce, ginger one ounce, warm ale three half-pints, or if pimento is not at hand spirit of nitrous ether one ounce instead. If in half-an-hour after the above has been administered no visible mitigation of the complaint exhibits itself, it will be necessary to repeat the dose, this time with a drachm more pimento. The belly of the horse should be well rubbed with a brush and moderate exercise given. Never allow the horse to lie down and roll, for by doing so when the spasm is on, the bowels will contract with cramp and become tied in knots, and we then have a case of twisted gut, for which there is no relief. In an hour after the above has been given, if no relief is afforded, the belly and sides should be rubbed with the following :—Mustard in powder eight ounces, camphor one ounce, oil of turpentine two ounces, water of ammonia one ounce, and three half-pints of linseed oil may be given as a drench. If the animal is costive with the colic, he should be back-raked, and enemas of warm soap and water with linseed oil injected every half-hour. This disease is often mistaken for inflammation of the bowels, which is caused by the general appearance being somewhat similar. If my readers will follow me in the following description of these two complaints they will be able to detect at a glance the difference between the two. In spasmodic colic we have the following symptoms : —Pulse natural or lower than its natural state, but accelerated and fuller during the spasm ; second, sudden in its attack but destitute of febrile symptoms; third, lies down and almost invariably rolls on its back ; fourth, legs and ears of a natural heat; fifth, rubbing the belly gives relief to the animal ; exercise evidently gives relief; seventh, intervals of rest ; eighth, strength hardly affected ; ninth, mucous membrane of the nostril of an ordinary colour ; tenth, lining of the eyelids of a natural colour ; eleventh, slight motion of the intestines unless by purgative medicine.

Now, mark the difference of symptoms of inflammation of the bowels; first, considerable acceleration of the pulse, but very indistinct; second, gradual in its approach, with febrile indications ; third, lies down but seldom, rolls on its back, starts on its legs suddenly ; fourth, legs and ears cold ; fifth, belly exceedingly tender, and when rubbed causes great pain; sixth, exercise increases the pain ; seventh, constant pain ; eighth, rapid prostration of strength ; ninth, the mucous membrane inside the nostrils very red ; tenth, lining of the eyelids unusually red; eleventh, peristaltic motion of bowels excited, with the anus hot. Pawing the ground is common to both complaints, but in cases of entanglement of the gut it desists from pawing. It is that portion of the intestines called the ileum, which by the horse throwing itself about during the continuance of the spasm, that becomes twisted and knotted together with astonishing firmness ; for this there is no cure, and death soon closes the scene. Horses that have frequent attacks of colic may be suspected of having stone in the intestines, most probably in the cæcum or colon. Sometimes they are of several pounds weight. Professor Pritchard showed me one this summer as large as a full-sized cocoa nut, which was taken out of a horse that had died of spasmodic colic. These obstructing the passage of the gut produce colic pains, and at other times, when exceedingly large, by pressing upon the mucous membrane produce inflammation. But as yet we know of no distinctly marked symptom to tell us of their presence, and no certain mode has been discovered for their removal. Another evil arising out of long-continued spasmodic colic is interruption of the intestines; this from long-continued spasmodic action on the ileum sometimes causes an inverted pressure upon the cæcum towards the stomach, which overcomes the natural action and forces this contracted portion of the intentines into a portion above it which retains its natural calibre. The irritation thereby produced increases the upward action, and causes still more of the intestine to be forced inward, until an obstruction of an insurmountable character is produced. We have nothing to indicate that this incurable malady has taken place but the long-continued pain.

INFLAMMATION OF THE KIDNEYS.

This is not a common complaint, yet occasionally cases of this kind crop up, and are usually produced by fever, and when completely formed the horse stands with its hind legs wide apart, and has an awkward gait in its walk. It withdraws from the pressure of the hand upon the loins, which also indicates an undue heat, considerably above that of its natural condition. When turned with moderate quickness it feels pain, and looks back wistfully at its flanks, as suppression of the action of the urinary organs takes place and is followed by a difficulty in voiding urine, which comes off in small quantities and is generally high-coloured, and not unfrequently mixed with blood. Strong efforts are made by the horse to void it in larger quantities, but at length it is almost entirely suspended. Hence it will be manifest that there is an affection of the urinary organs, but at first it will be difficult to say whether it is the kidney or the neck of the bladder. At this stage of the disease, according to Brown, the pulse is hard and accelerated; it soon after becomes small, although retaining its character of hardness. In order to find the seat of the disease, the hand must be forced up the rectum, and if the bladder (which is situate under the rectum) feels distended and hard, then it is certain that the disease is in the neck of the bladder. If, on the other hand, it is soft and feeling empty, with heat in the intestines over it, then there is inflammation in the bladder itself; but if there is no unnatural heat over it, then you may infer that the inflammation is in the kidneys. Musty or mowburnt oats and hay are often the cause of inflammation in the kidneys. Farmers in these hard times turn all their good oats and hay into money and keep only the inferior for their horses, and pay the piper accordingly. Another cause of this complaint is giving too strong doses of diuretic medicine, especially

if the medicine is largely made of turpentine. This
will bring on an attack of inflammation of the kidneys
as well as weakness in the parts. A sprain in the loins
by a horse falling with a loaded cart, or jumping short
in the hunting-field into a ditch with its hind feet,
causing a sudden check to the muscles of the loins, is
another cause; exposure to the cold rain, and being
allowed to cool and dry without being rubbed down,
will too often cause inflammation of the kidneys.
In this disease much difference of opinion is expressed
as to the treatment to be adopted; some advocate
bleeding, others affirm that bleeding does no good, but
this is certain that as much counter irritation should be
given with mustard as it is possible to produce. Spanish
flies should not be used for blistering in this complaint,
as they are a powerful diuretic, and a great deal of them
would pass into the system by absorption, and cause an
increase of the mischief. The horse should be kept
warm, plenty of cold water given it to drink, its food
should be mash, and the following given him three times
a day:—White hellebone one scruple, tartar emetic one
drachm, linseed-meal two drachms, made into a ball with
treacle. If the inflammation is in the bladder and its
sphincture we find the same symptoms; the urine is
voided in small quantities, and with great difficulty, and
in extreme cases there is a total suppression of urine.
When this takes place the bladder becomes exceedingly
inflated under the rectum, and may be easily felt by the
means advised in a former page. It is a spasm that
causes the neck of the bladder to contract, which is
produced by some acid substance which has been

generated in the system by the use of food of a heating
nature, forming a chemical compound of an acrid quality
of urine ; stone in the bladder will also produce this
disease. Some persons are so absurd as to administer
the tincture of cantharides by way of hastening the
season of horsing the mare, which is almost certain to
inflame the neck of the bladder. Some practical men
advocate bleeding until the animal faints for this complaint, which they say will cure it at once, but should
this not be done, the following should be given every
three hours : —Powdered opium one drachm, linseed-meal
three drachms, made into a ball or given in a drink. In
cases of mares being afflicted, the water can be drawn off
easily with the catheter, which would give great relief,
but with the horse it is difficult to pass the catheter, and
should not be attempted by anyone who is not a practical
man. Strong blisters should be applied at the same time.
In cases of stone in the bladder, we have no well-defined
symptoms, but the irregularity of the discharge of
urine with the occasional suppression of it, and fits
resembling spasmodic colic, are symptoms which
attend this disease and may lead us to suspect that
stone exists. To ascertain if it is really stone which
produces these symptoms, the horse should be thrown
on its back and the hand forced up the rectum, when
the stone may be easily felt, and if it is large then an
operation is necessary, which can only be performed by
a clever practical veterinary surgeon, but if the stone or
stones are small, they may be carried away with diuretics;
the best in cases of gravel is carbonate of potass and
digitalis ; three drachms of potass and one drachm of
digitalis may be given three times a day.

DIABETES.

This fortunately is not of such common occurrence with the horse as the human subject. It consists of an excessive discharge of urine, and is often the result of greed on the owner's part, many farmers selling all their good hay and oats, keeping only the inferior for home consumption, and in consequence have their horses taken with this complaint. The fungus of mouldy hay and fusty oats will produce irritation of the kidneys, and to mend the matter they often administer powerful diuretics, which cause inflammation with an increased action of the kidneys. The veterinary surgeon is then called in to cure that which ought not to exist, and indeed would not had they really studied economy and their own pockets, and kept good food for their horses. This complaint is very diffi-cult to cure, and the remedies must be with a view of lessening the undue action. Bleeding is sometimes resorted to, but this should not be carried on to the extent that it is sometimes in inflammation. I have more faith in strin-gent medicine, and counter-irritation; strong mustard blisters across the loins with the following astringent given three times a day will have good effect:—Wortle-berry leaf two drachms, catechu two drams, opium half a drachm. If it can be got green food and carrots should be given as well as bran mashes.

STALING OF BLOOD.

This is another disease of the kidneys, and nearly allied to inflammation in its symptoms, and always manifests itself with highly-coloured urine mixed with blood. Mostly the bowels are costive, and the following should be given :—Barbadoes aloes five drachms, cream of tartar half an ounce, powdered ginger one drachm, balsam copaiba thirty drops, to be formed into a ball. When this has operated, the following should be given once a day until the urine has assumed its natural colour :—Peruvian bark half an ounce, prepared kali two drachms, antimonial powder half an ounce, nitre in powder one ounce, balsam of copaiba a quarter of an ounce ; let the above be well powdered and given in linseed gruel, three ounces of linseed boiled in half a gallon of water until it is reduced to three pints. This treatment will generally cure this complaint in ten days.

WORMS.

Another thing which greatly troubles the horse and its owner is worms in the intestines. A variety of worms inhabit the intestines of horses, and when they become numerous, often prove injurious to the constitution. Although some writers say that they are not of much consequence unless they are numerous, yet the author's humble opinion is that an empty house is better than a bad tenant, and he would recommend that the sooner they are expelled the better. If there are only a few settlers they soon gather around them a numerous progeny, for where a single pair exist they will be like Paddy's bugs, become married and have large families, and in a short time they become a numerous colony. It is perfectly true that by what means they first effect a lodgment in the animal system is a problem yet to be solved, but it is equally true that naturalists have detected that these

o

parasites are formed male and female, and as nature formed nothing in vain, they must propagate in the ordinary manner of reproduction. Very much has been written about the parasite kingdom in relation to the animal economy of late years. I do not intend to enter fully into their organization, but shall be content to turn out the bad tenant, and be glad when I have done so. The general symptoms of being troubled with worms are loss of appetite, griping pains and rough coat, and tucked-up belly are symptoms of worms of the larger species, *lumbricus teres*, or long white round worm, very much resembling the long earthworm, and varying in length from five to ten inches in length. Itching of the rectum, evinced by quick twitching of the tail, and a small quantity of mucous, which hardens and has the appearance of white powder, at the anus ; this is indicative of the presence of *ascarides*, small needle-formed worms, which lodge in the larger intestines, and frequently find their way in great numbers into the cæcum. A third species, although of much rarer occurrence, inhabits various parts of the intestinal canal from the stomach downward; this is the tapeworm, which is known from its broad, flat, tape-like appearance, and consisting of many joints. This species is the most formidable and the most difficult to remove. In No. 3 of the Fifth Series of Science Lectures for the People, the following description of the tape-worm is given :—" There is one group of worms—namely, the *cestoidea* or tapeworm. Here we have a truly singular series of creatures. Most people have heard of such worms, but comparatively few have seen any.

There is one which is called *tænia medicanellater*; it is
the tapeworm which the human host obtains when it
eats underdone beef; it is the most common form of
human tapeworm. It is quite a delusion to think that
the pork tapeworm is as common as that derived from
beef." Professor Cobbold says, "I can speak quite con-
fidently on this point, because I have investigated this
subject very carefully. The beef tapeworm has four
suckers, but no hooks. The one from pork is recognised
by its head having a series of hooks in addition to four
suckers, *tænia solium*." The tapeworm is a most
remarkable creature; it consists of a head and a
segmented body, which is sometimes twenty feet long
or more; each of its joints or segments is what Professor Huxley would term a *zooid*; it is a sort of semi-
independent whole; in fact, a tapeworm is not a single
creature, but a multitude of creatures, all arranged
together in single file. You probably have made
acquaintance with those pretty objects which are found
on the sea-shore, the zoophyte or polypus, with its
numerous heads. Now, the compound polypus is a
colony of individuals, branching out like a tree; but the
tapeworm is a colony of polypus ranged together in a
single file like a regiment of soldiers, and thus one long
creature is produced by a number of little beings adhering together. Some 1200 individuals are here joined
together so as to form a colony. Professor Cobbold
says—" I will explain something specially peculiar and
interesting about the tapeworm. I have performed a
series of experiments which have resulted in giving us a
more perfect knowledge of the entire life, history, and

mode of development of the beef tapeworm. I will explain to you one kind of experiment I made. I took a portion of a tapeworm comprising several of the joints or segments towards the tail end, each of these joints when perfectly matured and ripe contain at least 30,000 eggs, therefore you can easily reckon up how many there would be in 12,000 joints, supposing all were mature. I took a number of these joints and put them into milk to make them easy of administration, and with the assistance of Professor Simons and other friends, fed a calf with them. Well, they went down, and the calf was none the worse apparently ; however, after a time it was evident that something had gone wrong, and what had taken place was this, some thousands of eggs had been swallowed, and of these eggs all that were perfectly ripe contained in their interior each a little creature called the six-hooded embryo. This small embryo has a round body provided with two needles in front, and a pair of hooks on each side; with the two little needles it bores, and with a pair of hooks it tears the flesh of the host. After the calf had swallowed the eggs, the shell of each egg was dissolved by the gastric juice of the fourth stomach, all the little embryo thus making their escape ; this, you see, was kindness to the embryo if it was unfair to the calf. The thirty thousand of little creatures, rejoicing in being free, soon made their way through the flesh of the host. The little calf did not succumb to these wounds, as the human bearer often does to the trichinæ ; by our assistance it recovered. Well, we calculated how long it would be before these little embryos would arrive at the higher level stage of development, and we had indications afforded us that it would be three months, so at the expiration of three months the calf, which was now a strong animal, was slaughtered in the cause of science and humanity, and when we removed the external parts it was found that the muscles, especially the superficial one, were filled with the higher larvæ of this parasite. The larva measle or bladder worm is called, scientifically, the *cysticercus bovis*; thus we reared in this calf many thousands of these parasites. Supposing we had sent this calf to market, what would have been the result? Every individual who partook of the veal, and who did not in cooking, raise the temperature to 1450, would, undoubtedly, have been liable to have developed in his interior the adult form of this particular parasite. How do we know that? We have experimental proof in various ways. A gentleman in India has lately had the courage to induce a Mahommedan boy to swallow some under-done meat of this description purposely, and the result was that the boy had the privilege of playing host to as many tapeworms as he had swallowed examples of this little *cysticercus*. Dr. Joseph Fleming brought over from India the largest specimen ever seen, which was taken from meat served out to our troops as rations. What happens when the measles are swallowed is this, the bladder-like part is immediately digested. These latter pass down from the stomach into the alimentary canal, a process of budding commences, and in three months the worm is fully developed. Such astonishing phenomena as these, are not the result of disease or accident; they constitute together the life cycle of a creature expressly organized to lead a parasite life. I have never yet heard of an English butcher who had ever seen one of these parasites, and yet I believe that at this moment at least 10,000 persons in this country are playing the part of host to these creatures. Butchers are profoundly ignorant in this respect. You will say, How do cattle get the parasite? I will explain : Millions of these creatures pass from their human bearers every day in this country, with other things that are vile, and make their way into the sewage, which it is now the fashion to spread over the land, far and wide, and are thus distributed by millions upon the delightful verdure on which our cattle graze." These eggs are thus often taken into the mouths of animals along with green fodder ; every egg swallowed from fresh sewage becomes a measle, and every measle that is in the flesh of the animal goes to market, and is thenceforth liable to be sold and eaten, and will afterwards become a tapeworm, providing the purchaser does not take the precaution of having the food properly cooked. Here is the value of reason—the animal neither reasons about it, nor does it cook its food ; if we would avoid these things ourselves, we must simply have the food well cooked. A temperature of 160°, if continued will be sufficient to kill trichinæ, whilst 140° will kill *cysticercus bovis.* The horse becomes affected with tapeworm in the same manner as cattle. When the symptoms we have pointed out are noticed, the groom should carefully watch whether worms are voided, to ascertain their existence. Still, however, they may be lodged in the intestines without being evacuated, and when there is well-grounded suspicion that they inhabit the body, a dose of some vermifuge should be given. This may consist of eight grains of calomel made into a ball, with oatmeal and treacle, or one drachm of powdered male fern may be given in its stead. For round worms the following may be given :—Calomel two drachms, rhubarb one and a-half drachm, soccoline aloes two drachms, ginger two drachms. If it is necessary to repeat the anthelmintic, then the following may be given :—Calomel one and a-half drachm, aniseed in powder half an ounce, powdered scammony half a drachm, to be given at night, and the following purgative in the morning :—Aloes five drachms, ginger two drachms, made into a ball with treacle. When the animal is infested with *ascarides*, the same medicine should be given as for round worm, but it frequently has not the desired effect. Indeed, I doubt if it is not the best practice to use injections at the first; these should be of linseed oil one quart, or aloes dissolved in warm water one ounce; this should be used in combination with the above medicine. If the existence of tapeworm is apprehended, then the following should be given after the calomel and male fern :—Turpentine half an ounce, castor oil two ounces, gum-arabic in powder one ounce, made into a ball with treacle. Warm mashes should be given for a day or two afterwards. It seldom happens that the animals are entirely expelled with one dose, therefore it is necessary to repeat the doses, for unless we are certain that the entire animal has been discharged, our work is not half complete, as if only one link is broken off and left in the intestines, it will be generated into a perfect worm, they having the property of reproducing the parts of which they have been deprived. So much for the tapeworm. May my reader never have the trouble to expel them.

THE BOTS.

These are another and common kind of worm, or, more properly speaking, they are the larvæ of the gadfly, *æstrus equi.* There are two species of gadfly, hence we have two species of bots, which are known under the distribution of red bots and white bots. Their natural history and habits are exactly alike. Horses may be affected by bots without being materially injured by them, but I cannot agree with Mr Bracy Clark that they are essential to the well-being of the horse, or that they were destined by Nature to act upon the food in the stomach by trituration, or as pepper does in the human stomach. Like every other part of the animal's body this organ is so admirably constructed that in its healthy condition no artificial aid is necessary to enable it to perform its office. If, as Mr Brown says, the theory of Mr Clark was correct, what would supply the place of those parasites during the time of year that the grub assumed its perfect condition? In *post-mortem* examinations I have made, proof has not been wanting of their not being inoffensive as Mr Bracy Clark supposed. One subject I opened four years ago—a black cart mare, the property of Frederick Neame, Esq., of Macknade House, Faversham, which died from violent inflammation, and the stomach, upon opening it, was found covered with these parasites. So thick were they that you could not see one particle of the mucous membrane of the stomach, they forming a complete lining. Upon removing the parasites the mucous membrane was eaten into holes, in some places nearly through the substance of the stomach. They were also found through the entire intestines so numerous as to leave no doubt that they were the primary cause of the animal's death, and although they were so numerous in the animal no one suspected their existence, as none had been seen in the evacuations. The progress of this disease generally manifests itself slowly; the horse becomes hide-bound, its coat becomes rough and unhealthy, it loses flesh and strength, although it feeds with its usual appetite, and frequently it has a short tickling cough. The bot, as I have said before, is a species of the gadfly, which may be observed in the months of July flying actively about the legs of horses in the fields, or sticking fast to their ribs when ridden along a road. These are the females depositing their eggs in the hair of the horse, to which they adhere by a glutinous substance with which they are surrounded, and in a few days the eggs are hatched, and the minute grubs are set at liberty. This is done by the horse licking itself, and the little grubs adhering to the tongue of the horse are carried into its stomach with its food. These small caterpillars are provided with a small hook on each side of the mouth, by means of which they cling pertinaciously to the cuticular portion of the stomach, and so tenaciously do they adhere that the hook will break before they leave their hold. These pests contrive to locate during the winter and to the end of the following spring on the mucous of the stomach, by which time they attain a fully-grown size, and must then, according to the law of Nature, undergo a new transformation. They quit their hold of the coating of the stomach and are carried along with the food, from thence they pass into the intestinal canal along with chyme, and are at length discharged with it.   These caterpillars thus evacuated seek an appropriate place in the ground, where they assume a chrysalis condition ; remaining in this state for some weeks they at length break out from their swathing and assume the form of a perfect insect ; immediately after this the male and female pair. The latter becoming impregnated sets about seeking an appropriate place to deposit its eggs, which in imitation of the parent they fix on the hair of the horses' legs, to become in their turn a pest to the horse.   The treatment I have given elsewhere for worms should be adopted for these pests.

According to my promise in a previous page I will proceed to give a few hints about buying horses, and will endeavour to expose some of the tricks that are resorted to by unprincipled horse-copers and dealers.   Little do novices in horse-flesh know or think how many tricks are resorted to by dishonest dealers to conceal the defects of a horse and take in the uninitiated.   To exhibit a few of these will be the aim of this paper, and if it is not pleasant to those who make a living by the practice of unfair means to deceive the unwise, I offer no apology to them, for if the cap fits they may wear it.   The first thing for a man about to purchase a horse is to attend to its form, which differs materially in various breeds,

and its good points will depend upon their adaptation
to the particular kinds of work. The head in all the
breeds should be fine, broad between the eyes, and
tapering towards the nose. The jaws should be clean,
and not possessing too much flesh, the eyes full and
sparkling, clear and lively, the nostrils rather large and
open, and of a clear red colour, the space underneath the
jaws should be roomy and free from any glandular
swelling or lumps, the ears should be well set into the
head and pricked forward, but not large, which is
generally a sign of a soft-hearted horse. The neck should
be well curved, lightly formed rather than muscular, and
considerably arched beneath at its union with the jaws.
The shoulders should be high and sloping, the withers
should be of a medium breadth, and not too high, as it
will be found that high-withered horses are generally
narrow in the chest, which is always a bad point in not
allowing sufficient scope for the lungs to play, and is
never so pleasing to the eye as a broad expanded front.
Still some horses have proved both hardy and good in
point of action with narrow chests, but these have had
depth to compensate for the want of breadth. However,
there is a medium in the chest of a horse; great width
is generally accompanied with want of action, and such
horses are better used for cart or farm purposes. The
back should be short and somewhat arched across the
loins, the chest deep and the ribs expanding, especially
between the last rib and the hip, so as not to admit of a
hollow between them. This is called well ribbed up; a
loose-ribbed horse is always unpleasant to the eye if it is
not a physical defect; no feeding will fill up a horse in

that quarter, nor can a horse be pleasing to the eye that has not good hind-quarters.

They should be round and full of muscles, the hips well developed; a low rump is a characteristic of an Irish horse, and is termed amongst dealers a "goose rump;" many blood horses have this formation. Avoid the purchase of one so formed, as they seldom have good action; horses long in the quarters are seldom serviceable. If a horse is required for field sport always buy one short in the quarters, which is indicative of all good leapers. The thighs should be muscular and extending to the back, from which to the hoof should be clean, flat, and sinewy. The back part of the thigh should have a considerable bend, as a straight-legged animal seldom possesses good action, although there are exceptions to this rule. Avoid those that are "cat-hammed," viz., with their hocks nearly touching each other, see that the fore-legs are muscular down to the knee, and otherwise well formed as I have described in the hind-legs. The fore-feet should be nearly circular, gradually increasing as they descend toward the sole; their inclination outward should not be so great as that of the pastern. The chances are that feet that slope too much forward are diseased or liable to it; besides this obliquity throws the animal too much on its heels, which produces tenderness of the parts and straining of the back sinews. The position of the legs and feet, or what may be termed their setting-on, is a most important point. Viewing the horse from the front, the horse's legs should be as near straight as possible, its feet

neither inclining to the left or right, as feet turned
outward are very liable to cut and trip, and the action
is seldom good or agreeable to the eye, having an outward
movement, and thereby losing ground at every step.
Horses with an inward inclination of the feet are said to
be " pin-toed " or " pigeon-toed ; " these generally throw
their feet outward, exhibiting the sole of the foot whilst
in action. Such horses have generally a laboured action ;
they soon tire when upon a journey, as the fatigue is
equal to a third, more or less, of the journey. The fore-
legs should be well set under the fore-part of the shoulder,
affording ample support to it. Such as have their legs
placed forward have neither support nor action ; when
the legs are viewed sideways or profile, they should be
nearly straight, but when horses have what is called
" calf knees," that is the knees sunk backwards, and with
the shank-bone sloping forwards, it is a certain sign of
weakness, and such horses will more easily knock up
when on a long journey; yet I do not recollect ever
seeing a " calf-kneed " horse with a broken knee. The
hind-legs should be either straight from the hock down-
wards, or have a slight inclination under the belly.
Horses so formed are for the most part low in the rump,
and will throw out their legs well under them when in
action ; on the contrary, horses that throw out their
legs are disagreeable to ride and seldom good workers,
Horses that stand with their legs much under them,
and at the same time droop in the quarters, may be
suspected of being diseased in the kidneys or spine,
and should be carefully examined upon that point.
While doing so on no account let the dealer's servant

held up the horse with a bridle or stand on rising ground; this should be especially attended to whilst examining the legs. It is invariably the practice of dealers when exhibiting a horse to place it so that its fore-legs are on the highest ground; this is done to hide the defects of the formation or disease of the horse's legs and feet. Never let a dealer's groom throw the reins over the horse's head and hold it back with the curb while he touches it under the belly with a long whip, which has the effect of putting it on its mettle, and therefore it hardly knows where it places its feet, consequently it will bend both its knees and throw out its feet more than it does in its ordinary style of going. These wily servants take care to always bring the horse to a stand with its fore-feet on the highest ground, which makes it advance its legs so as to conceal any knuckling of the knees or pastern.   If they object to let the horse go and stand naturally, be sure that it is a screw, and has some disease they are anxious to conceal, and that by their placing it with its fore-feet on the rising ground they are anxious to conceal its knuckling at the knees or pastern joint, and by doing so they give a "groggy" animal all the appearance of soundness. The first point for a purchaser to attend to is the head at the crown, to ascertain if it has had the disease I described in a former page, called *poll-evil*; examine its nostrils carefully, pinch both nostrils close together so as to make the horse blow its nose when you loose your hold; this will enable you to find out if the horse is "plugged," and if it blows out of its nostril a pleget of tow or cotton wool be sure it is a glandered subject. Take particular notice if there is a foetid smell from its nostril; this is a point the coper cannot entirely do away with; the horse's breath should be as sweet as new-mown hay. If it has a foetid smell and a discharge from the left nostril only then it is glanders without a doubt, but if the discharge is from both nostrils you may conclude that it is a case of *nasal gleet.* The coper will tell you that it is only a cold the animal has, but depend upon it if you buy it you will have bought a handful of trouble. The tongue should be particularly looked at to ascertain if it has met with any injury from the bit. If you find that it has the appearance of having been cut across, make up your mind it is a puller; if, when examining the mouth, there is a ropy saliva from the mouth hanging in strings, be sure there is a wound in the mouth, and examine carefully to find out if it is of a recent date or an old and cankered wound. Next look carefully at the eyes for *gutta serena* and other affections of blindness; see that the withers are not fistulous; carefully scrutinise the knees by lifting up the legs and bending the knees in an upward form, if they have been broken ever so slightly, this will reveal the scar. If you find a small scar, look to the manner the horse wears its shoes, and if you find the toe worn away and the other part of the shoe in good condition, look out for a stumbler, and a stumbling horse is liable to come down at any moment. Examine the legs carefully below the knee for splint and grogyness by placing the horse's feet on the lowest ground; look carefully to the pastern joint, and notice particularly if

both bones are alike on each leg; feel carefully round
between the joints of the upper and lower pastern, and
if there is any enlargement no doubt there is a ring-
bone forming.   The hocks should be carefully examined for "thorough-pin." Notice if the point of the
hocks are swollen or what is called "capped," if they
are look out for a kicker.   See if there is any enlargement about half way down the hock on the hinder
part of it, if there is he has a "curb," and it is sure he
has weak hocks.   Examine narrowly the inside of the
hocks for bone spavin ; the writer has known some
dealers point to a large bone spavin and say the animal
had a fine bony hock.   Descend to the feet and examine
for grease, look out for sand-crack in the horny substance of the hoof; see that there is no canker separating
the substance from the fleshy part of the foot.   Look carefully under the heels of the shoes for a small stone ; if
you find one, be sure the horse has been "beaned."
This is done with a lame horse:—The bean is placed
with a pair of pincers under the heel of the
shoe of the sound foot; this causing the animal
great pain makes it tread heavily on the lame
foot, so that it has the appearance of being
sound, whereas it is actually lame on both fore legs.
A "beaned" horse has always a low action, and the
dealers will say it is only a natural low gait of action.
Disbelieve all their excuses, and err on the safe side by
rejecting the purchase.   Sweeping as my readers may
think of this condemnation, it is unfortunately too
true, that this class of men are not to be depended
upon, and considering the risks that they themselves

arc liable to, it is not to be wondered at. If the legs show any signs of having been bandaged a well-grounded suspicion may be entertained that all is not right. Pay particular attention to the state of the animal's wind, for if the animal is touched in the wind he is sure to be "loaded" before going into a fair. Perhaps my readers may misunderstand the word "loaded." This is another trick of the unprincipled professional horse coper. When they have a horse broken-winded which they wish to sell, they generally contrive to get some one to make a "swop," *i.e.*, exchange ; by doing so they steer clear of the law and the animal is not returnable. When they are about bringing the horse out of the stable they load him, this is done by making up a quarter of a pound of shot into a ball with soap, and putting it down the animal's throat. This loading is done to bear down the animal's stomach and give temporary relief to the animal's lungs, and many a poor man has found out next day that he has exchanged a useful horse and given several pounds to boot for an animal that is not worth fifty shillings.

Another trick which is carried on to a considerable extent is the art of "bishoping." This is a trick which takes its name from an unprincipled dealer of olden times, who was supposed to be the first man who resorted to this piece of roguishness. Bishoping a horse is done by throwing a horse and putting a large wooden roller into its mouth while the operator files down its teeth ; then, with irons made for the purpose, he proceeds to burn the centre of the teeth, making them resemble the natural marks in a young horse, so that a

P

horse that has fresh legs and is nearly as old as Old
Parr, in an hour is brought out as a seven-year-old and
sold as such. Old horses are generally sunk in the eyes,
but after the coper has bishoped his animal he is quite
up to the mark to make the horse have a younger appearance, so he proceeds to another trick known as
"puffing the glims." This is pricking the hollow above
the eyes with a needle to cause local inflammation and
swelling of the part. The swelling fills up the cavity
above the eye, and gives the horse a younger appearance, but this only lasts for a day or two, and often ends
in ophthalmia, from the inflammation affecting the optic
nerve. Other dealers who have young horses wish to
pass them off as older than they are for the extra profit
they obtain, and many three-year-old horses are sold as
four-year-olds, and the writer has known them passed
off as five-year-olds. This is done by punching out their
sucking teeth and lancing their gums above the tusk;
when the suckers are punched out the cutters soon
make their appearance, and by lancing the gum it falls
back, and in a few weeks the tusk has made its way
through, so that the mouth of a three-year-old has
much the appearance of a four-year-old colt; and many
persons not well up with the mouth of a horse are
imposed upon in this manner. This trick is known in
the trade as "yorking the horse." In purchasing a
horse the physical signs of age must be also looked
to, because a young horse may have been too early
put to hard work, and to that extent that it is to all
intents and purposes an old horse in strength and action;
when heated by being trotted or galloped all his infirmi-

tics disappear, but these will re-appear whenever it is again cooled down. A horse with an upright shoulder is more fitted for driving than riding, a sloping shoulder is best adapted for riding, for they have generally better action and less of its own weight to sustain on its fore legs; a long-necked horse is generally admired for its graceful form, but we consider this a fault, as such are generally weak and are predisposed to roaring. Short-necked horses are for the most part clear-winded, but one of medium length should be preferred. Horses whose limbs have been fired should never be purchased only at a small price, as it is a sure sign of disease, although many horses work well after being cauterized; indeed scores of hunters and race horses have been subjected to this operation. Thanks to the French, the old system of firing will soon disappear, as their patent firing apparatus can be used without the aid of fire and irons, and Professor Pritchard informs me that he has fired upwards of 200 animals with it and has not had one slough, which is a very great recommendation for it, as with the old iron and the most careful operator it was impossible to prevent some from sloughing. When the cornea of the eye is of a yellowish tinge it is indicative of liver complaint; this being observed, turn up the lips and notice if the under portion of the lips are of the same colour; if so avoid the purchase of the animal. If the coat of a horse stares it is a sure sign that the animal is not in good health; it will be noticed that their dung is either hard, dark-coloured, fœtid, and slimy, or thin and washy like a cow. When not disturbed such animals have a languid and sleepy appearance, but dealers take care before showing them to temporarily rouse them from their lethargic condition by what they term "figing" them, that is by forcing ginger up the anus, putting salt into its mouth, and an application of the whip. Go through a dealer's stable, and as soon as the voice of the dealer is heard all the horses are on the alert; they know he does not carry his whip in his hand for nothing. Who ever saw a dealer without a whip ? No, without his whip he would be like a pump without a handle. No sooner does the master or one of his men enter the stable than the horses begin to raise their tails, champ at their bips, and assume all the appearance of good health and spirits ; in the meantime the dealers use all their claptrap eloquence to induce the novice to believe the animals are the best in Britain, and they are too often successful in inducing their intended victim into that belief. The writer once heard one of these men say " That he did not mind what they called him as long as they did not call him a fool, for this world was made up of sharps and flats, and as there were always two flats born to one sharp, there was always a good stock to work upon, and there was no credit in doing a fool." There are so many gentlemen who fancy that they do know what a horse is, and think they cannot be done, who are quite disgusted when they get an animal from one of the professional copers which turns out a rank screw. When I use the term dealers in such a sweeping condemnation, I would have my readers understand that I refer to copers at fairs, and the advertising gentry ; that there are honest dealers is without a doubt, but they are men who have a name at stake, who will have their price for a horse, and do not deal after the Jewish manner of asking twice as much as they intend to take. It is by far the best plan for purchasers to go to such men who will let them have a horse on hire with the option of purchase; if they have to pay a little more at the first (which is doubtful) they have a fair chance of trying the animal. In buying a horse the hand should be drawn over the ribs and the fingers pressed firmly between them; if the skin appears tight and unyielding it may be inferred that the animal is hidebound, and consequently labouring under some internal disease. I would most particularly draw the attention of the intending purchaser to the fetlock joints of the horse, and if he finds a mark of a cut which may be only an inch long or it may be some inches, situate parallel with the shank bone, and immediately below the pastern joint; if such a mark is found it is certain that the horse has been nerved, an operation which is performed by cutting a portion of the nerve away to render a horse workably sound which has an invariable attack of navicular disease, such horse should be instantly neglected. In examining the foot, if the sides of the hoof are marked with circular depressions running parallel with the coronet, it is certain that severe inflammation has existed at some time in the sensible portion of the foot and is consequently liable to a return of it at any time after a little over exertion. See that both fore feet as well as the hind ones are of an equal size, and ascertain that they are quite cool and equally so; attend to the sole, see that it is of its proper shape; thrush can be detected by the smell, besides the other symptoms

which I have already described. As the feet of horses
are of such importance, I would advise every one to
acquire a knowledge of them, and to do this there is no
better plan than to attend daily a well-employed shoeing-
forge, and for a small gratuity the smith will point out
the different formations of the feet that come under his
observations. If he has had experience he will be able
to point out readily the indications of disease ; he will
also see why different formed feet require that the shoes
should be modified and adapted to the peculiarity of the
structure or probably existing disease. The next important thing to study is the wind, for it is this point
that the coper knows well how to patch up for twenty-
four hours, which is long enough for his purpose ; study
all that I have said upon the different complaints of the
lungs.   The wind may be tested by what is known as
coughing the horse, that is by pinching the windpipe immediately behind the jaw. If the horse gives a long sharp
cough it is an indication that it is sound in that respect,
but if the cough be short and hollow it may be inferred
that the horse has unsound lungs.   Let gentle pressure
of the windpipe be frequently repeated in order to fully
test this, and be sure to do this with your own hand, as
dealers know that by compressing the windpipe with one
hand and the forefinger of the other, the horse is forced to
cough while doing so and produces that shrill sound considered a test for good wind, by the air rushing through
the limited aperture.   Having satisfied yourself in this respect, proceed to watch the flanks in breathing; if the belly
of the animal swells out and the inspirations and the ex-
pirations are regular, it may be reasonably inferred that

the animal has good wind, and its lungs are sound, but if they are irregular and stops before it is completed, with considerable drawing in of the flanks extending up the sides so as to shew plainly the ribs, then it is certain that the horse is unsound, or, as it is termed, broken-winded.

The third and final test is to trot the horse smartly and watch the motion of its flanks, and observe if it utters a noise in breathing with considerable blowing; if it does, reject the horse at once. To examine the horse to ascertain if it is a roarer, whistler, or piper, place it with its side against the wall, hold its head up with the left hand, and with the right hand give it a sharp blow on the ribs, or touch it smartly on the belly with a stick. If it utters a grunt at every blow, it is a sign it is a roarer; if it jumps about in consequence of the blows, sobbing, and drawing its breath quickly, this will be found an indication that it is a whistler or piper. For testing all diseases of the lungs there is nothing like giving a good gallop round a field, beginning slowly and increasing the speed until it is at its top speed, then stop short, dismount, slacken the girths, and place your ear against its chest upon the wind-pipe, and the least defect in the lungs will be apparent. Consider no time wasted that is spent in testing the wind of the horse, and indeed all points connected with its health. There are so many points to be looked at and so many things to look for in buying a horse, that if the purchaser is in a hurry he is sure to overlook some important part. Having satisfied yourself that the wind is all right, next stand behind the animal and carefully scrutinize the prominences of the hip bones, and see if they are on the level, and especially

mark the round bones which are situated a little posterior
to the prominence of the hip. This is liable to lameness
from blows, strains, and other causes. If there is any
fault here, there will be a wasting of the muscles, and
the defect will be more readily detected when the horse
is in motion. If any symptom of lameness is observable,
pass the hand over the spot, and heat is sure to be found
in the part; it may be probably verified by applying
your nose to the part, for in all probability there will be
the smell of some liniment which has been applied.
When examining a horse, never let the dealer's man
hold its head high, nor place its feet on rising ground,
because, as I have said before, while a horse stands in
this position the defects (if he has any) of its fore-legs
will not be apparent, whereas if it stands with its feet on
the level ground, if the limbs have been shaken from hard
work, they will exhibit a tremulous appearance, the
knees will be more or less bent, and the heels will not
rest firmly on the ground as they ought to do. Horses
that have been hard worked will have the fetlocks of the
hind legs bent and relaxed, and the natural elasticity of
the tendons and ligaments will have departed. The horse
that is termed groggy, when standing in a quiescent
state, will be found with a leaning posture over the fore-
legs, the feet of which will be further under the belly
than the upper portion of the limbs, and the entire limb
forming a flat semi-circle with the knees at the extreme
point of the curve. In looking at the action of a horse
see that its feet are lifted high, and that all four feet
clear the ground. Some horses have high action with
their fore-feet, and would scarcely knock over a sixpenny

piece with their hind-feet. See that the horse throws out its feet freely and lightly, stand in front of it when it is trotted, and notice if it has an inward gait of action ; if so, it is sure to strike one leg against the other and be liable to fall, and will be a subject for throwing splints. If the horse has an inward gait of going, chalk the inside of its hoof and then trot it ; if the chalk marks are on its fetlock it will be a brusher, but if on the knee joint it is a speedy-cutter, which is the worst form of cutting, as the horse is apt to knock one leg from under it with the other, the result being a severe fall and broken knees to the horse, and perhaps a broken neck to the rider or driver. After the horse has been examined in front, stand behind it whilst being walked and trotted, and you will then be able to detect the least uneasiness in its going, and ascertain if it is a loose goer. Some horses have an outward gait of going, and look as if they tried to throw away their feet at every step; this kind of action is objectionable, as a horse with such an action soon tires on a journey. Horses with a short confined step can never have good action, and are always disagreeable to ride. In walking, the knee should be moderately bent, but only sufficiently so to enable the horse to walk clear of the stones and other objects he may meet with on the road, and when the foot is set down the foot should fall flat, so that the toe does not strike the ground first. The legs should be thrown straight out, bearing neither to the right or left, nor should the sole be seen by a person standing on either side. In the larger-sized horses the step should be lengthy and regular, in the smaller-sized smart and springy, and in either case the horse should tread with its hind-feet upon the footprints of the fore-feet. If the horse steps short with his hind-feet, look for bone spavin in the hocks. Wide hipped horses sometimes tread on the outside of the footprint of the fore-feet, have generally a shaky action, and are unpleasant to ride. Wide hipped horses are almost always heavy in the shoulder, and are therefore more adapted for harness than saddle. Thoroughbred horses generally have low troting action, and therefore are not good hacks upon the road, but having a more springy action are much more pleasant to ride. Blind horses always lift their feet high, and have a high uncertain action, therefore when trying a horse which has high action examine its eyes carefully, for perchance it is owing to defective sight that it lifts its feet so high. When speaking of horse coping, I used the term advertising gentry. No doubt most of my readers have had their attention drawn to advertisements in the papers of the following style :—" To be disposed of immediately, a pair of handsome bay geldings, 16 hands high, six years old, quiet in double and single harness, constantly driven together, the property of a gentleman who is leaving England, a warranty given, and trial allowed.—Apply to coachman for price, &c., at ———— Mews, Hyde Park, London." This is called doing the heavy to catch a flat, and is generally done by the so-called gentlemen who buy on commission. It requires three to carry out this trick to perfection, and it is often done. Coper No. 1, 2, and 3, look out for horses of showy action with fresh legs and broken wind, they then engage a stable, hire a carriage and showy harness; the advertisement is put into one of the principal papers. Coper No. 1 engages apartments in a fashionable quarter, and takes the name of Col. Somebody. Coper No. 2 dons a suit of livery and is for the time being Col. Somebody's coachman. Coper No. 3 assumes the humble grade of helper, which he is in truth. The trap being set the spiders wait for the fly, who in general turns up in the shape of a young Swell, who thinks he knows, and who has never learned the Spanish proverb, " That the man who knows, and knows that he knows, passes a happy life; the man that don't know, and knows that he don't know, may pass a very tolerable life; but the man who don't know, and don't know that he don't now, is a fool indeed." The swell arrives at the stable and Coper No. 3 opens the door and touches his hat, (they are already very polite), the Swell asks Coper No. 3 " Is this the stable where the horses advertised are to be seen?" at the same time showing the advertisement. " Yes sir'" is the reply. " Are you the coachman ?" " No sir, coachman is gone to the house for orders." " Oh, then, you are helper I suppose," at the time, sliding a shilling into Coper No. 3's hand, and thinking he shall get some information out of him respecting the horses. " What sort of horses are they? are they quiet ?" " Yes, sir ?" " Do you know anything wrong about them ? If you tell me and I buy them I'll make it all right with you." " No, sir, I don't know of anything wrong, but if I tell you you won't let out to master or coachman." Swell thinks he is in for information this time, and promises not to speak

about what he is told, and Coper No. 3 tells him he has
heard coachman say that when they are fresh the near-
side horse do pull.   Coper No. 2 now puts in an appearance with livery boots and breeches on, and in a great
hurry, " Jim, put the harness on at once, govenor wants
the landau at once." Then noticing Swell for the first
time, says " Good morning, sir," touching his hat in the
most approved style.   Swell, " Oh, you are coachman, I
wanted to have seen these horses out but you seem in
a hurry."   Coper No. 2 says " Yes, sir, master has
had bad news and wants to catch the train, but, sir,
you might jump on the box with me and ride round to
the door, then you will have a chance of seeing how they
move, and could make arrangements with master, when
you could come and see the horses tried."   Swell thinks
this a good chance, and gets on the box and is driven
slowly round to the lodgings of Coper No. 1, who
is quite the gentleman, and is extremely sorry that
he cannot spare time to shew him the horses, but
the fact is his dear son is taken very ill at Eton,
and he is off to see him, but perhaps he would
not mind riding in the carriage with him to the
Great Western station, and then, James, the coachman,
will drive him back to any part of the town he wishes.
The bait is taken, and in jumps Swell and Coper No.
1, Coper No. 1 taking care to keep up a conversation,
and pointing out the action of the horses as they turn
the corners.   150 guineas is the lowest price Coper No.
1 can take, he gave 200 guineas for them from Lord
Tom Noddy, and only offers them at the price as he
is anxious to get them a good home before leaving

England to join his regiment. The fly is well into the web, and before parting on the platform a cheque is given by Swell, and a receipt and warranty given by Coper No. 1, and Coper No. 2 receives orders to take the horses home to Swell's stables. Coper No. 1 takes a ticket to Westbourne Park instead of Eton, then a cab to the bank, the cheque is cashed, the carriage sent to the coachbuilder, the hire paid, the stables are left, and the lodgings also. The horses are taken to Swell's stables and a sovereign given to his coachman, and Coper No. 2 gets one from Swell. The horses are given as much water and hay as they can eat and drink for a day or two, then Swell takes his new purchase out into the park for a drive, and sends them along at a smart rate up the side of the Serpentine to the Magazine, when he puts his head out of the carriage window and says " John, what is the matter with the horses, they make an awful noise?" John says " I don't know, sir, but I think they must be broken winded." The horses are then taken home, and Swell goes to lodgings of Coper No. 1 and finds that he left them the same day he bought the horses, the stables are next tried to find the birds flown, and Swell then learns for the first time that he does *not* know all. In a day or two after a carter-looking man with a smock frock on, has heard that Swell has a pair of broken-winded horses for sale, and as he has a bit of land, he thinks he can work them on it, and offers £10 for the pair, which Swell, being disgusted with his purchase, takes, and the horses are then taken, not to work on the land, but next time to be advertised as

brougham horses, or are put into Tattersalls or St.
Martin's Lane, to be sold as the property of a gentleman. Coper No. 2 looking after them and having in
his pockets some weighted balls, which he takes care to
give the animals before the show commences.   Coper
No. 2 runs up the horses until he thinks he has
attained enough for them, when they are knocked
down to some novice, who thinks because that horsey-
looking gentleman bids so much for them he has not
given too much by giving a fiver more.   There is
another class of land sharks in the horse line, and they
are as dangerous as the common coper.   These are the
guinea hunters, or gentlemen who buy horses on
commission.   Many of them when they know a gentleman is in want of a certain class of horse will go to a
fair or to some coper, and buy a good-looking screw
for a few pounds; they will then send it to stand at
livery at some respectable livery stable.   Coper No. 2
is again called in, but this time he takes the part of a
gentleman, and Mr. Commission-hunter introduces Mr.
Flat to Mr. Sharp, who soon sells him a miserable
screw, Mr. Commission taking his share of the
plunder, and departing in peace.   When the horse
arrives in Mr. Flat's stable, they find that if they
have bought a horse they themselves have been sold.
There is still another class who are the most heartless
of all the horse coping tribe; they are men who sell
horses upon commission.   If they have a wealthy man
they will sell his horse fairly, because they think they
can make him pay, but let a man who has come down
in the world and is forced to sell his horse and

carriage fall into their hands you will just see the difference of their treatment. They will let the horses stay in the stable and never try to sell them until a large bill has run up for expenses, then they look out for a customer and when they have one, will go to the owner and tell him things are very dull and that he cannot get a bid for them, but as the captain wishes to part with them he will give 50 or perhaps 100 guineas for the pair and keep them himself in case a purchaser should turn up. The money is handed over, and the next day the animals are shewn and find another master at about £300, thus fulfilling the proverb that when a man is down every one will kick him. Yet the men who do this trickery would be shocked if they were accused of dishonest dealings. Scores of this kind of cases could be quoted, but I think I have said enough to show that a man when buying a horse at a fair or from an advertisement, should not do so with his eyes shut, and although the groom is considered ignorant, yet many gentlemen would have sounder and better studs if the advice of their grooms and coachmen were taken in the selection of them. That there are many ignorant grooms and coachmen there is no doubt, but I contend that there are as many intellectual men to be found among them as in any other class, and if in my writings I have given umbrage to any of my readers by my plain speaking, I am sorry for so doing, but as my motto has been " Proud to praise, yet not afraid ‚to blame." I could not be truthful unless I blamed the groom for many things, and the masters for as many more. No bad workman ever had a good tool, and no bad master ever got a good man. If, on the other hand, my writings have proved beneficial to my readers, and by them I have added one jot more comfort to the horse, my studies are not in vain.   Remember always the merciful man is kind to his beast. Treat them kindly and you will find many more good horses than bad ones. In conclusion, I have to thank all those gentlemen who by their kindness to me have enabled me to quote so much from their writings for the information of my readers, and above all, I hope to pay a life-long tribute to the memory of the late Sir Thomas Moncrieff, who encouraged me as a boy in my studies with the solicitude of a tender father and friend, and but for him I should not have been able to sign myself,

Yours faithfully,

A STUD GROOM.

NORWICH : ARGUS WORKS, ST GILES' STREET.   LONDON : 84 FLEET STREET.